CW01677324

Jewellery

Sylvia Wicks

Macdonald Guidelines

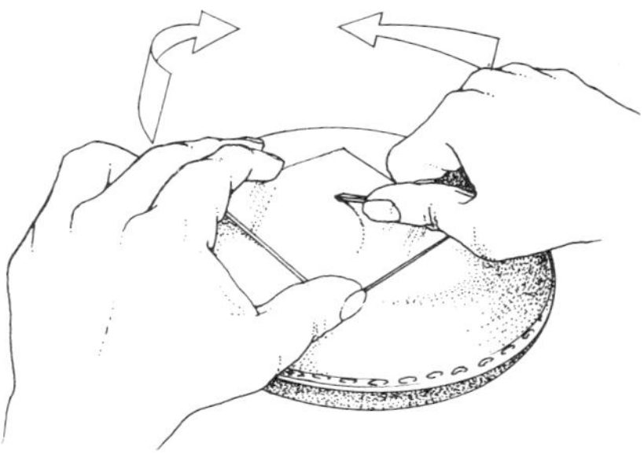

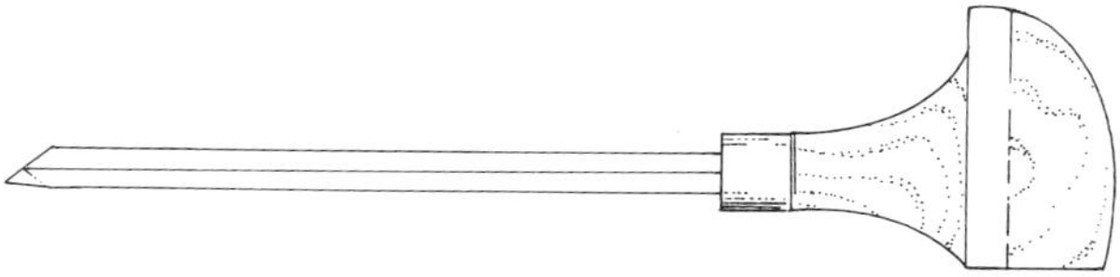

Managing editor
Chester Fisher
Series editor
Anne Furniss
Designer
Patrick Frean
Production
Philip Hughes
Picture research
Lynda Poley

Made and printed by
Waterlow (Dunstable) Ltd

ISBN 0 356 06006 3

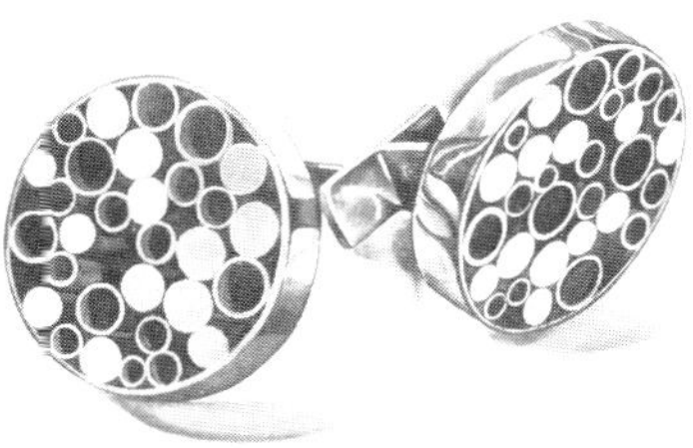

Contents

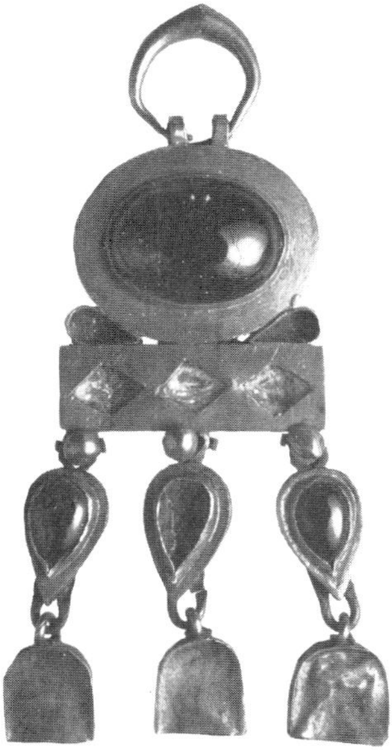

First published 1976
Macdonald Educational Ltd
Holywell House, Worship
Street, London EC2A 2EN

Reprinted 1978

The first jewellery

The rings, brooches, bracelets, necklaces, pendants and ear-rings worn today differ little from those of early civilizations, and the basic metal working techniques of the early craftsmen were similar to those used by modern jewellers. Steel tools now replace bronze or flint implements and electric machinery has reduced the time needed to complete a piece of jewellery; but the techniques remain almost unchanged.

What is jewellery?

Early jewellery was for self-adornment and was made of objects judged to be beautiful, rare or precious. Since things of value were used in its construction, jewellery was considered to be evidence of riches. People wore jewellery also to indicate official position, social status or affiliation. In some cases it became a mark of success. For example, in several primitive societies, a necklace of teeth or claws from a wild animal showed the hunter's skill.

A mystical or religious significance was attached to particular pieces. Jewellery was thought to acquire supernatural powers of protection if made with magical marks or shapes, or if made when the stars were in a favourable position.

Today the reasons for wearing jewellery are similar. Officers of the armed forces have insignia to show their rank, a mayoral chain indicates the civic status of the wearer, and members of an organization all display identical badges to show their affiliation. Instead of a necklace of teeth, a hero of our society is awarded a medal in recognition of bravery.

Certainly, a large gold and diamond brooch is an indication of wealth, and also reckoned to be a good investment. This is because the durability and rarity of the gold and stones guarantee that the value of the jewellery will be retained.

The mystical association of jewellery survives in the wearing of charm bracelets and crosses, and, just as the ancient Egyptians wore amulets and talismans to guard against evil spirits or danger, some people carry St Christopher medals to protect them while travelling.

◀ A Chelsea pensioner, veteran of World War I, wearing his war medals.

▶ One of the earliest pieces of jewellery ever found. This shell necklace is believed to date from 20000 B.C. It was found in a grave near Rome.

The earliest jewellery

The first jewellery was made by Stone Age people who collected such things as shells, pebbles, and teeth. They made holes in their selected objects and strung them together to form necklaces. In a grave near Monaco, some of the earliest pieces were discovered. Archaeologists found three necklaces of fish vertebrae and estimated that they were made between 25000 B.C. and 18000 B.C. In eastern Europe, diggings revealed a communal grave in which each occupant had a necklace of ivory beads.

As man progressed from 15000 B.C. to 5000 B.C., so he advanced technically. He became more skilled, firstly at drilling stones, then at carving and polishing them; and he began to arrange the objects on his necklaces in order of size. This deliberate arrangement may have been man's first efforts at jewellery design.

Early peoples turned from hunting to farming and they began to trade. It was no longer necessary for one man to produce all his own requirements. As a result, specialists in various fields evolved. Technology began to develop more quickly as metalworkers and other craftsmen were able to concentrate their efforts in their particular areas of interest. And so the first precious metal jewellery industry began.

Sumerian jewellery

The earliest examples of gold jewellery were discovered in the excavations of Ur, a Sumerian city established in the Euphrates Valley in about 3500 B.C. Archaeologists unearthed men's pendants, necklaces, pectorals (chest plaques), ear-rings, and bracelets for the wrist and upper-arm. Among the collection of women's jewellery were rings, ear-rings, necklaces, bracelets and diadems (head ornaments). The diadems ranged from single gold bands to ornate crowns. Some of the most outstanding pieces were in the tomb of Queen Pu-Abi. She was found wearing an elaborate head-dress made of tubes of lapis lazuli and rows of paper thin leaves of gold. She also had on large hollow ear-rings and a bead necklace.

▲ The Sumerian jewellery found at Ur is about 5,000 years old. The necklace, dress pins and head ornaments are made of gold and cut stones. The ear-rings are loops of gold. The Sumerians based their designs on both natural and geometric forms, including beech and willow leaves and simple rosettes.

By the time of the Sumerians, stone carving had developed sufficiently for stones to be shaped to suit a particular design. Turquoise, obsidian, cornelian and lapis lazuli were commonly used. As local supplies became scarce, many of these stones had to be imported from the Persian Gulf.

Most forms of jewellery known today were made and worn by the Sumerians 5,000 years ago.

The art of the metalworker

By 3000 B.C., people had learnt to isolate gold. They may have panned for it, or refined it from ore.

The method of panning for gold has been in use for centuries and is still used by some prospectors today. In panning, a mixture of gravel, soil, and sand thought to contain gold is shovelled into a shallow bowl. Water is continually swilled over the contents until the lighter materials are washed away, leaving the heavier gold.

The golden fleece

To refine gold ore, people smashed gold-bearing rocks. They ground the pieces to a powder, mixed it with water and then poured it over a sheepskin. The heavy gold deposits lodged in the natural oils of the fleece, while the water carried away the rock particles. The gold-impregnated fleece could either be dried out and the gold particles shaken from it, or burnt and the gold retrieved from the ashes.

The gold dust had to be made workable. Heat was directed onto the gold particles on a charcoal block. Under a hot flame the gold melted, then fused together to form one piece. The naked flame of a fire was not hot enough to fuse gold. Extra oxygen had to be present to get the high temperature required. Egyptian tomb paintings indicate how this was done. They show craftsmen using a mouth blowpipe over an open fire. The blowpipe, a reed with a clay nozzle, resembled the metal tube sometimes used by jewellers today for blowing across a gas flame. Later, bellows were used to fan the fire in a clay furnace.

Ancient skills

When cool, the fused gold was beaten out to form sheets. Initially, a pebble and a rock served as hammer and anvil. Gradually, tools of flint, copper and bronze appeared and, later, iron and steel implements were made.

Ancient craftsmen achieved a high degree of skill. They were able to hammer gold into sheets so thin that they were almost transparent. To do this, layers of gold and specially prepared skins were beaten together. The resulting sheets, known as gold leaf, were used for gilding.

▶ This 19th-century illustration shows a man prospecting for gold. Panning is a method of separating gold which has been used from the earliest times.

Jewellery-making techniques in use by 2000 B.C.

The early craftsmen first cut metal with a chisel-like flake of flint. They already knew how to file stones by rubbing them with grit, to polish them with crushed emery powder, and to drill them with copper or bronze tools smeared with emery powder and oil. They soon adapted these techniques to metal, and found that string or fibre would cut if it was coated with the abrasive emery powder and drawn back and forth across the object.

Early jewellers formed relief patterns in metal with various shaped punches and engraved lines with a flake of flint.

They developed stamping techniques and hammered lead against gold to push it into the recesses of a mould.

At first, pieces of metal were riveted or tied together, but people soon learned to solder. They made wire by rolling metal between two stones, and created delicate patterns with fine wires and tiny granules of metal. They also learned to cast metal.

Soon, the craftsmen began to add colour to jewellery with stones. By this time, most of the techniques in use today had been developed.

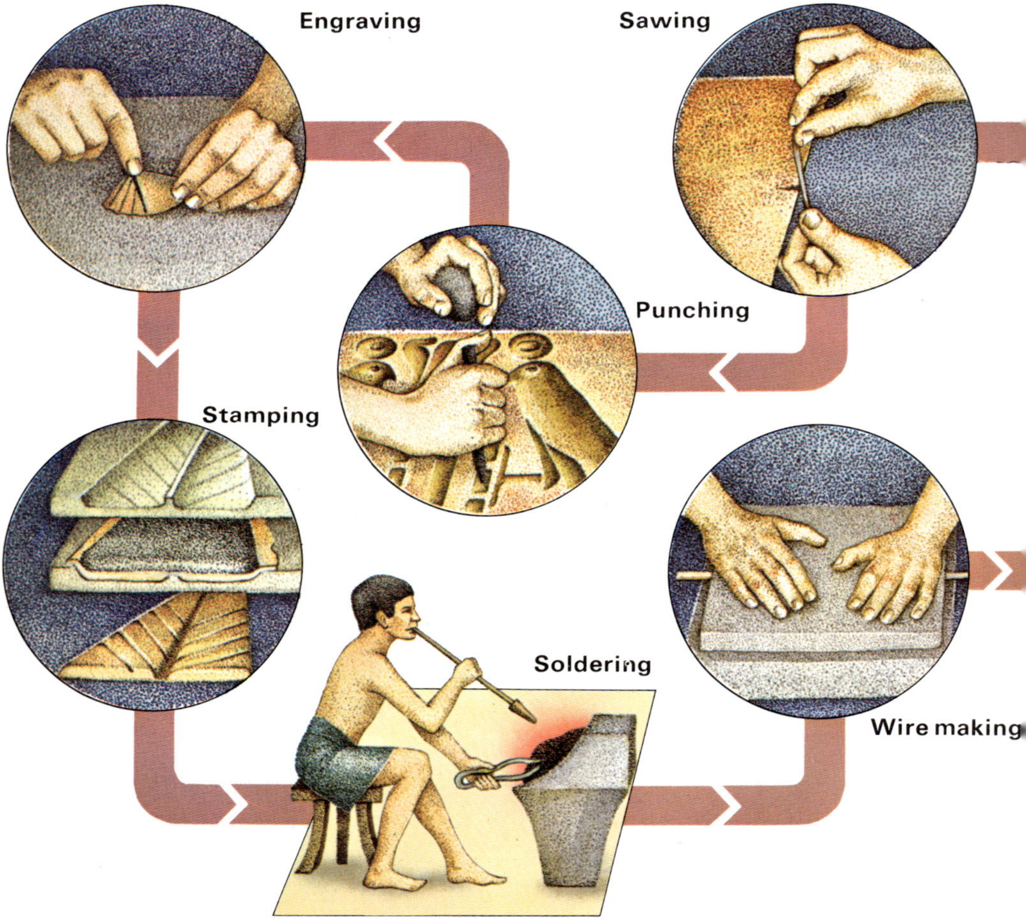

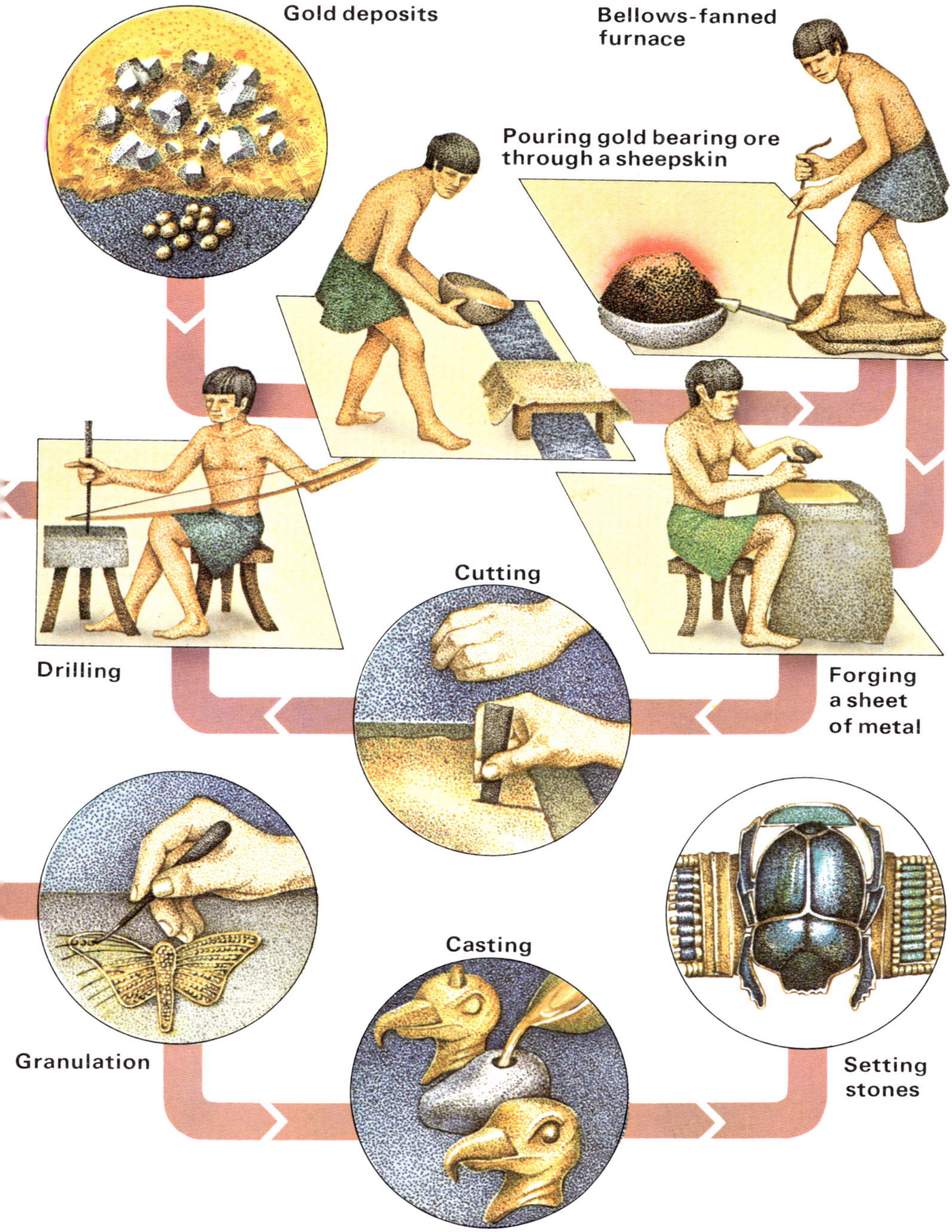
Gold deposits
Bellows-fanned furnace
Pouring gold bearing ore through a sheepskin
Drilling
Cutting
Forging a sheet of metal
Granulation
Casting
Setting stones

Early fashions

In the Nile Valley, the Egyptians wore jewellery both as ornament and for protection from harm. It was thought that snakes, scorpions and other vicious animals kept away evil spirits. Falcons, scarabs and cowrie shells preserved the wearer from various dangers. Certain geometric symbols were supposed to bring wealth, long life and other personal benefits. These motifs occurred on all forms of jewellery and became stylized as they were used again and again by craftsmen.

Gold and colour

To the Egyptians, gold reflected the power of the sun ; it was plentiful within their empire and so was used lavishly.

The area in which the Egyptians contributed most at this time was in the use of colour in jewellery. They advanced methods for inlaying stones, and employed the rich colours of lapis lazuli, cornelian and turquoise to represent sea, earth and sky. Faience, a method for producing glass imitations of stones, developed at this time, probably as a result of the scarcity of the real thing. Lapis lazuli, for instance, had to be imported from distant Afghanistan.

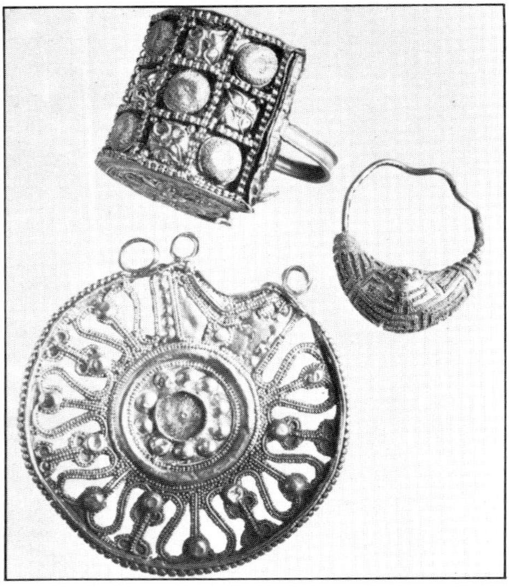

Minoa and Mycenae

In contrast to the Egyptians, the Minoans, living on the island of Crete in about 2000 B.C., used comparatively few stones in jewellery. They did, however, carve seals from stones and eventually became expert at depicting animals and symbols in cornelian, agate and rock crystal.

Initially, Minoan designs were based on rosettes, spiral patterns or marine and hunting motifs. Metal-working techniques were simple and, since gold was a scarce commodity, many pieces of jewellery were fashioned from gold foil or fine gold wire.

The highest levels in Minoan craftsmanship were reached during the years from 1700 B.C. to 1375 B.C. One of the skills at this time was the stamping of beads from thin gold sheet. The gold workers made these relief beads in such large numbers that it may be considered an early form of mass production.

The Mycenaeans from mainland Greece conquered the Minoans in 1400 B.C. They did not impose a style of their own on the

◀ The way in which the Etruscans made the granulation decoration for their jewellery is a secret which was buried along with the Etruscans themselves. Modern craftsmen can only guess how the effect was achieved. These examples are a pendant and two ear-rings.

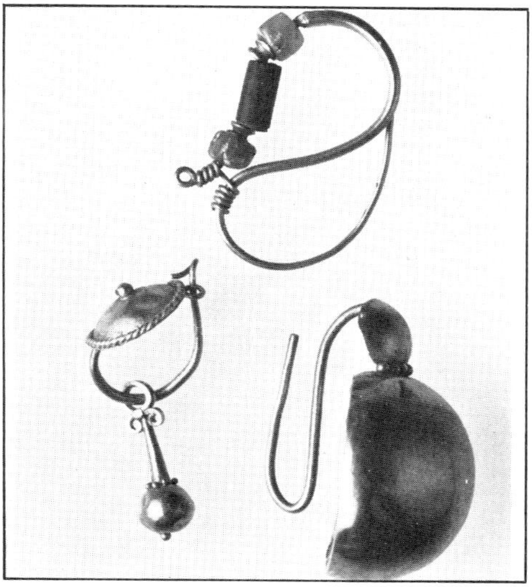

◀ By Roman times, fashion had become an important influence in the development of styles of jewellery. Shown here are three different styles of Roman ear-ring.

jewellery already being produced, and relief beads remained the most typical form of jewellery.

Early beads were strung from a bar at the top of the bead giving a fringe-like effect to the necklace. Later, holes were drilled through the body of the beads enabling them to be threaded in denser formation.

The Phoenician influence

Phoenecia was originally surrounded, and therefore influenced by, the civilizations of Egypt, Sumeria, and the Aegean. In the 13th century B.C., the Philistines and the Israelites invaded Phoenicia and forced the inhabitants to withdraw to the coast. Being excellent seamen, the Phoenicians soon set up trade routes and colonies, and effectively opened up the ancient world. By bringing the artistic developments of one nation to the notice of another, they played an important part in the spread of design and craftsmanship.

The dictates of fashion

The early Greeks were modest in their production of jewellery, mainly because Greece did not have deposits of metal and had to obtain supplies from her colonies in Italy and Russia.

The decoration of the early period was geometric. Gradually, trade with the Phoenicians led to designs based on naturalistic motifs and mythological subjects.

The real advancement of Greek jewellery resulted from the conquests of Alexander the Great. Greece then had access to gold from the conquered territories, and the demand for jewellery increased as members of the new and wealthy merchant classes began to acquire collections of jewellery.

Stones began to be used in Greek jewellery. First the deep red garnets, sometimes emeralds imported from Egypt, and gradually cornelians, agate and rock crystal were included until the jewellery of this period (the Hellenistic era) was magnificent.

Fashions began to dictate more frequent changes in styles of jewellery. For instance, the boat-shaped ear-ring of the classical period lost popular support and a hoop ear-ring of twisted wire or hollow tube became the most desirable style. For a short time, fashionable Greeks wore stud ear-rings, but then the pendant ear-ring gained favour and became more and more ornate as the fashion continued to be supported. Necklaces and rings underwent similar changes.

The secret of granulation

For 400 years from the seventh century B.C., the Etruscan civilization of northern Italy produced jewellery unsurpassed in its technical achievement and beauty. A method was evolved for decorating the surface of work with hundreds of tiny grains

of metal lined up to form patterns. The secret of this technique, known as granulation, can only be guessed at by craftsmen today.

A popular ornament with the Etruscans was the fibula, a cloak fastening resembling a safety pin. The craftsmen at the time used every known technique to decorate these pieces, including the finest granulation.

The influence of the small city state of Rome expanded through central Italy absorbing the Etruscan civilization. The large army required for such an operation was costly to maintain and, as gold was by this time an international currency, all available supplies were required to support the army. This meant that, for about 300 years, Roman jewellery did not progress.

▲ This gold fibula shows the sophistication of Etruscan craftsmanship. It is hollow and about 18 cm long. The decoration is granulation.

The era of Roman jewellery really began with a change in the political system at the start of the Imperial period, about 27 B.C. Unlike the Etruscans, the Romans showed a preference for simple lines and their jewellery is notable for its lack of ornate decoration.

Finger rings were the most popular form of jewellery. Men and women wore many rings at a time, often on each finger and, sometimes, several fine rings on one finger. The Romans were the first to use rings as a sign of betrothal.

◀ A Greek necklace of gold from the fourth century B.C. The hanging buds and heads are hollow beads decorated with filigree and granulation.

▶ Roman rings showing a variety of styles and techniques. They are a ring with a knot of Heracles; a gold ring set with an engraved seal; a gold ring of *opus interrasile* (an open pattern cut with a chisel); a ring set with a coin and a ring set with garnets and sapphires.

Development of style

Emperor Constantine established Byzantium (Constantinople or Istanbul) in A.D. 330. The Byzantine Empire survived until around the 15th century, but the height of its influence was in the sixth century when it had amassed great wealth, including vast quantities of gold.

Constantine was the first Christian Emperor and the jewellery of the time reflected the current religious feeling. It was ornate in design and complicated in construction. *Opus interrasile*, the open chiselled work practised by the Romans, was developed with great precision by the Byzantine craftsmen.

Under Charlemagne, Emperor of Europe in A.D. 800, Christianity strengthened and the art of the goldsmith was almost exclusively patronized by the Church, whose influence lasted to the Middle Ages. Also at this time, the burying of jewels with the dead was stopped, so the only surviving examples of jewellery from the ninth and tenth centuries are the pieces in collections of cathedrals and religious orders.

By about the middle of the eleventh century, the monks could write. Records of work were kept and, for the first time, particular pieces of jewellery can be attributed to individual craftsmen. Another important advancement was the training of lay craftsmen by abbey goldsmiths. These people worked on a freelance basis when the pressures of work forced the monks to commission pieces outside the abbey. By the end of the twelfth century, there were sufficient numbers of such craftsmen to enable them to form a guild.

Twelfth-century jewellery was primarily functional. Sculptural buckles and brooches of many different designs were

▲ Byzantine craftsmen perfected the technique of *opus interrasile*. This seventh century gold ear-ring is an example of their work. It also shows a chased bird design.

typical. This was probably the result of both the style of clothing, which was a long-sleeved, high-necked tunic of two layers, and the rather unsettled times.

Jewellery was restricted to the nobility by law. For instance, in France at the end of the 13th century it became unlawful for commoners to wear pearls and precious stones, belts or circlets of gold and silver. So, under the exclusive patronage of the royal houses and religious orders, jewellery became primarily ceremonial.

Trade unions

The guilds, which had been gathering strength, were consolidated. In France, rigid conditions were drawn up to maintain the high standards of the craft. Metals used for jewellery had to be of better quality than that used for coinage. Imitation stones, pastes, or coloured foil backings used to give semi-precious gems a better appearance were forbidden; and regulations prohibited the mixing of fresh water pearls and salt water pearls on the same piece.

In London, there was a powerful secular guild of goldsmiths by the middle of the twelfth century. By 1300, the wardens of the craft were officially recognized by Act of Parliament and given responsibility for assaying vessels of silver. Edward III incorporated the London guild in 1327 under the name of "The Wardens and Commonalty of the Mystery of Goldsmiths of the City of London".

Charlemagne's talisman is said to contain relics of the True Cross. Buried with Charlemagne in 814, it was rediscovered in 1000, then held by the cathedral until 1804, when the canons presented it to the Empress Josephine to wear at her coronation.

A love of luxury

By the beginning of the 14th century, there had been a change of fashion at the French courts in both clothes and jewellery and a new love of luxury evolved. The religious and functional jewellery of the earlier years was replaced by jewellery encrusted with stones and richly decorated with stylized foliage and translucent enamels. Silver ap-

◀ One of the important metal-workers of the twelfth century was Nicholas of Verdun. This gilt bronze buckle, thought to have come from his workshops, shows a king and a queen in bas-relief. The sculptural treatment of a functional piece of jewellery is typical of the Middle Ages.

peared more frequently. Under the influence of the gothic architectural movement jewellery became more sculptural.

In England, following the French decree of the 13th century, Edward III forbade commoners to wear jewellery of gold, silver or precious stones, but squires and merchants with sufficient assets were not included in this law.

Spanish laws were much stricter and only the reigning monarchs and infantas were entitled to own precious stones, gold, or silver.

With such restrictive laws in force, the goldsmith's art was almost totally directed to the production of royal jewels.

The age of chivalry

This was the great age of chivalry and the many orders, guilds and associations which grew up devised badges to identify their association. Some of the famous societies which today still use the original badge of membership are the Order of the Garter, founded in England by Edward III, the Order of the Golden Fleece, which became the most esteemed order in Austria and Spain and the Order of the Elephant in Denmark.

When the short doublet became fashionable in the early 14th century, belts and buckles became an important form of jewellery for both men and women.

During the 15th century the status of jewellery changed from being a symbol of power and position to a fashion accessory. Women began to wear dresses with low-cut necklines, so pendants and necklaces appeared more frequently and rosaries were made in more ornate styles.

The pinched sleeves of the 14th century were replaced by wide loose cuffs in the 15th century, so bracelets again became

fashionable. By the end of the 15th century, with clothing more closely fitting, precious stones were sewn into the material to supplement the jewellery.

Both men and women throughout Europe wore gold chains. Particularly heavy chains fulfilled both decorative and currency needs. Each link was made to represent one unit of exchange and could be removed to pay for goods or services.

Another innovation of the period was the parure, which was a set of matching pieces of jewellery. A parure usually consisted of a pendant, necklace and headdress, but it might be extended to include the buttons on a garment.

The first designers

In the Gothic era of the 14th and 15th centuries the goldsmith began to emerge as a creative artist as well as a skilled craftsman

▲ This painting by Cranach dating from about 1530 shows his wife wearing the heavy gold chains which were typical of the period.

◀ This seventh century Anglo-Saxon clasp is part of the treasure found at Sutton Hoo, Suffolk, England in 1939. It is an outstanding example of the Barbarian skill with coloured stones and its typically geometric design is inlaid with stones and glass.

▶ A parure worn by the Infanta Isabella Clara Eugenia, painted by Sanchez Coello about 1570.

and individual pieces of jewellery began to be associated with their maker. But it was not until the Renaissance in the 16th century that the jewellery designer emerged as distinct from the craftsman. This may have occurred because the goldsmith's workshop was considered an ideal training ground for those wanting to become painters or sculptors. Famous artists such as Donatello, Botticelli and Albrecht Dürer began their careers as apprentices to goldsmiths. Later, the German painter Hans Holbein, designed jewellery for Henry VIII of England.

Virgil Solis, an engraver from Nuremberg, was probably the first to sell his designs. Delaure, a Frenchman employed in Strasbourg, circulated drawings, and pattern books soon became common throughout Europe. Also goldsmiths frequently trained in one city and worked in another. For these reasons the origin of some pieces of jewellery is difficult to determine.

▲ A typical Renaissance jewellery design. Many designs such as these were circulated in Europe in the 16th century.

▼ A 16th century goldsmiths' workshop.

◀ A gold Spanish corsage of the 17th century set with emeralds. It is typically delicate and based on the floral motifs popular in Europe at the time.

▼ The workmanship in the Canning Jewel is fine and inventive. The torso is a baroque pearl and the body, scimitar and shield are decorated with stones and enamels. Stones are used in a new way: instead of being added to make the piece appear richer, they are used to highlight a line or exaggerate a shape.

Jewellery for women

During the Renaissance, jewellery began to be the perogative of women. Men tended to wear richly embroidered clothing.

Elizabeth I of England, Philip II of Spain and the Medici family of Italy became the major patrons of the jewellery craft. But the greatest jewellers were to be found in Germany. In 1562, Erasmus Hornick of Nuremberg published a book of designs that showed a new and original approach to the traditional brooch and pendant. The subjects were mythological figures and parts of the body were often depicted by a large baroque pearl. Probably the most outstanding example of this new movement is the Canning Jewel.

The variety of jewellery forms again broadened in the 17th century with the change in fashion to flowing gowns. Many designs of this period were inspired by exotic flowers. Knots and ribbons were combined with the floral theme and resulted in jewellery with a light, open appearance.

Design begins to broaden

The style of jewellery is always dictated by the style of dress. The 18th century was the age of calculated elegance, with low necklines and three-quarter-length sleeves, so necklaces and bracelets were displayed to advantage. In the first half of the century, the delicate floral and ribbon themes in symmetrical designs continued in favour, but these were later replaced by asymmetrical designs with shells, scrolls, volutes and flowers in a colourful and extravagant style which came to be known as rococo.

By the middle of the century, the new emerging middle classes were seeking to emulate the jewellery styles of their social superiors. As they did not have the money to do so, the time was right for the development of substitutes.

In England, Christopher Pinchbeck discovered that an alloy of zinc and copper appeared similar to gold. All types of jewellery were produced in this metal, which became known as pinchbeck. Glass was cut like stones and these stones, called pastes, were produced in vast quantities.

New forms of jewellery that appeared at the time included the stomacher, a large bodice ornament, shoe buckles, and the chatelaine, a belt attachment to carry useful household items such as keys, seals and scissors.

◀ Useful household objects were hung from a chatelaine clipped to the belt.

▶ The art of diamond mounting was developed so that a stone could be set with very little metal showing. These 18th-century rings display the diamonds to advantage.

The first cheap jewellery

In the 19th century the growing middle classes demanded a greater variety of jewellery. The Industrial Revolution led to the development of mass production methods that provided large quantities of cheap jewellery.

Under Napoleon, there was a short revival in classical jewellery, but later, styles tended to be representational and based on sentimental and romantic themes.

Towards the end of the 19th century the jeweller, Fabergé, inspired the jewellery trade with a new originality and paved the way for the Art Nouveau movement.

▲ Fur clip by Fabergé. Fabergé's skill and originality in his use of materials and techniques soon won him important awards. He made few pieces of jewellery, but his ingenious use of stones and materials for visual effect instead of commercial value led to a new quality in jewellery.

◀ Pendant in gold and enamel by René Lalique. Lalique was probably the most outstanding of the Art Nouveau jewellers. His interest was in producing works of beauty, irrespective of their value. Inspired by nature, he worked in many combinations of metals, wood, horn and amber. But he excelled in the use of enamel on jewellery.

▲ "Eye of Time" by Dali. The watch face is blue enamel and the tear falls from a ruby. With the broadening of the concept of jewellery, many prominent artists experimented with their own ideas.

▶ Bracelet by Andrew Grima, one of the outstanding designers to emerge from the 1961 International Jewellery Exhibition. His spontaneous designs include a variety of textures, stone and materials.

New ideas

The Art Nouveau movement had faded by the outbreak of World War I. During the war, very little jewellery was made, but in the following years, clients demanded ostentatious, value-for-money pieces that demonstrated their wealth. Consideration was not often given to the design.

One great influence on the broadening of design in the 1920s was the Bauhaus School in Weimar, Germany. Its director, Walter Gropius, attracted a team of creative and original workers from all fields of art and craft. The traditional barriers between the disciplines were broken down and the resulting designs were well-balanced.

As a result of the Bauhaus experience, geometric forms became popular and jewellers chose materials that added to the quality of their design rather than to the money value of the jewellery.

World War II caused another break in jewellery production. After the war, artist-craftsmen began to emerge as creative designers and innovators. Most of the jewellery houses still provided high-quality, expensive items from stock or as special commissions. It was the artist-craftsmen who experimented with new techniques, offered for sale jewellery sometimes considered daring or absurd and finally lifted jewellery from the bounds of traditions.

As a result of the creativity of the artist-craftsmen of many countries, the appreciation of jewellery was extended to include pieces of any value, any material, any form and any style. A judgement of the value of the piece was at last based on the quality of the design.

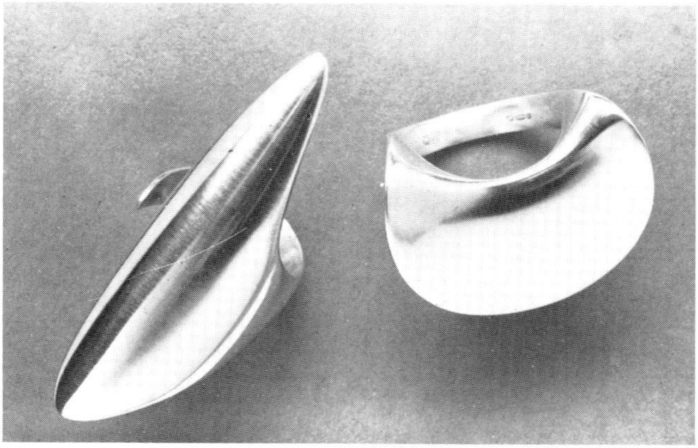

▲ Rings by Nanna Ditzel and Henning Koppel designed for the Danish jeweller, Georg Jensen. This firm is famous for its well-proportioned, simple, sculptural shapes.

▼ Pendants by Emmanuel Raft. The technique of casting enables Raft to give the silver a completely original quality. Fragments of black opal emphasise this effect.

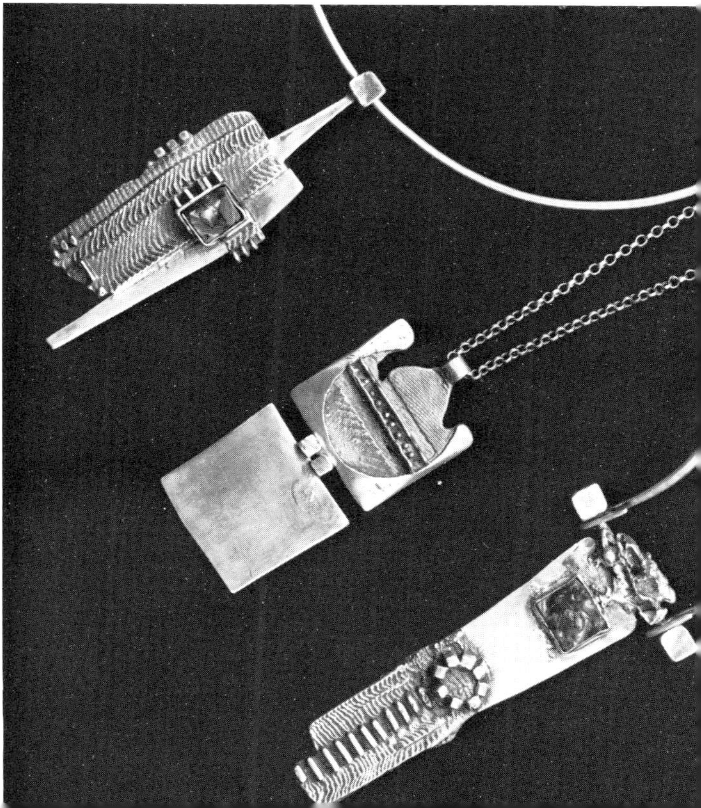

Jewellery today

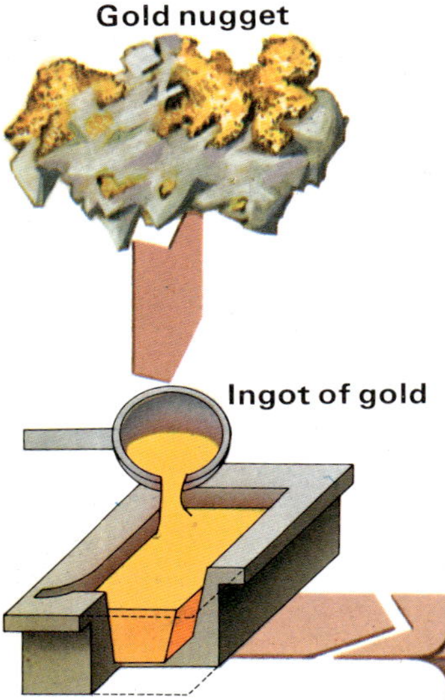

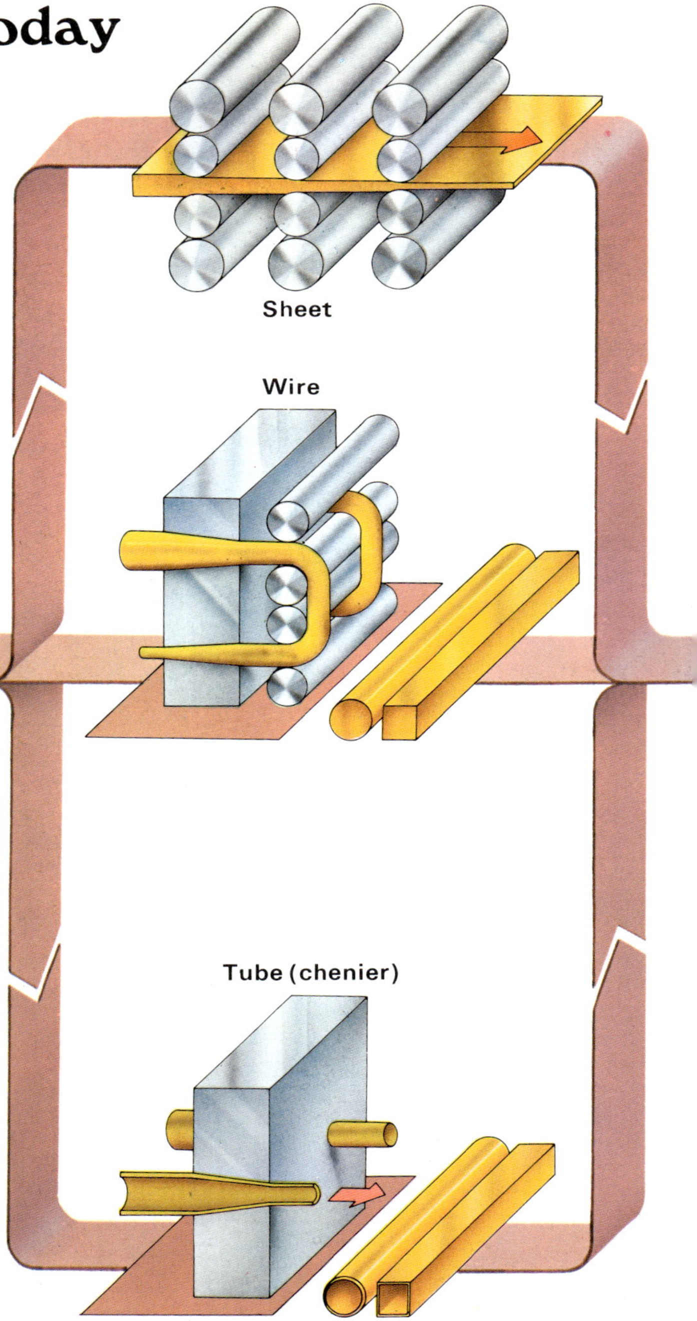

From a nugget to a ring
Gold ore is first isolated mechanically, then refined chemically or electrolytically and cast into ingots. The fine gold ingot is melted and alloyed with other metals to produce an alloy that may be harder, of a different colour, or cheaper, yet still retaining the essential appearance of gold.

The new alloy is made into sheets of various thicknesses, and wires and tubes of different sizes and shapes.

The metal is usually bought by one of three types of manufacturer:
1. the prestige jewellery house or small hand-made workshop.
2. the artist-craftsman
3. the mass production workshop.

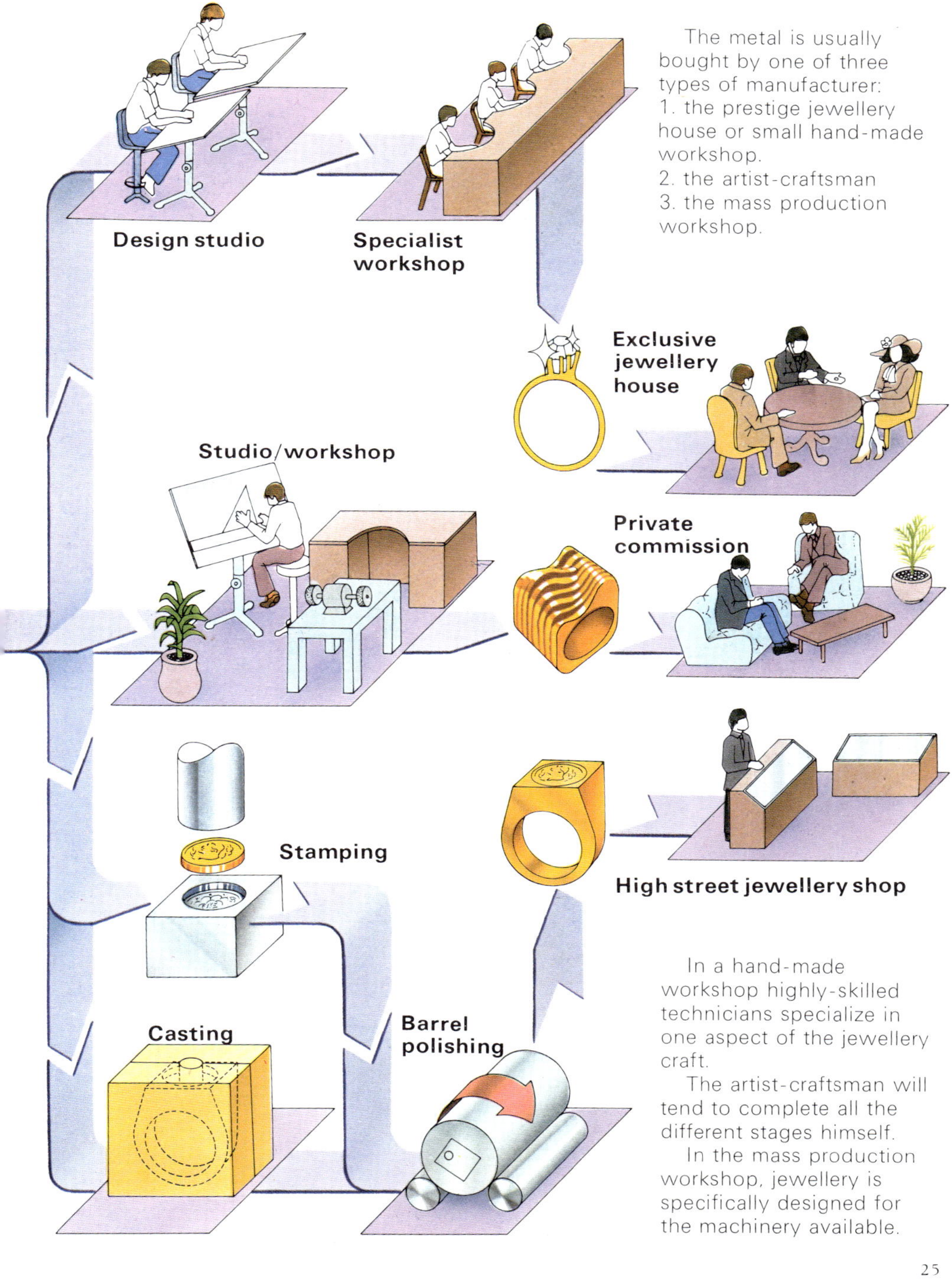

In a hand-made workshop highly-skilled technicians specialize in one aspect of the jewellery craft.

The artist-craftsman will tend to complete all the different stages himself.

In the mass production workshop, jewellery is specifically designed for the machinery available.

Gold and silver production

The popularity of gold jewellery increased after the sensational gold discoveries of the 19th century. The gold rushes in California, Klondike, South Australia, Victoria and South Africa attracted many individuals hoping to make a fortune.

Gold is found in veins (lode gold), along river beds (alluvial gold) and in deposits deep below the earth's surface. These deep deposits, known as reef gold, were only discovered about 65 years ago. The finely distributed gold particles were probably once along river beds that have since been covered over by the movement of the earth's surface.

The first prospectors panned for gold. Later, the gold digger made a long wooden box with a ridged base. He filled the box with sand and gravel from the river bed, then pumped water through the loaded box. Rocking the box allowed the flowing water to wash away the lighter gravel and sand. The heavier gold particles lodged in the bottom.

Most of today's gold is mined by large commercial organisations. In the search for alluvial gold, power-driven shovels dig over dried-up river beds and floating dredgers lift material from the beds of rivers or lakes. Or strong jets of water break away the exposed banks of ancient streams.

Reef gold is expensive to produce because it is so deeply deposited. The deepest mine, the Robinson Deep, Johannesburg, goes down to about 2,550 m. The Monro Velho in Brazil is nearly 2,300 m. below the surface, and the workings in the Kolar district of Mysore, India, reach depths of 2,100 m.

Today, few mines work solely to dig for silver although many did in the past. Silver is generally deposited with copper, so the large, commercial copper mining companies produce silver as a bi-product.

Mass production

The jewellery available now comes mainly from one of three sources. It may be from

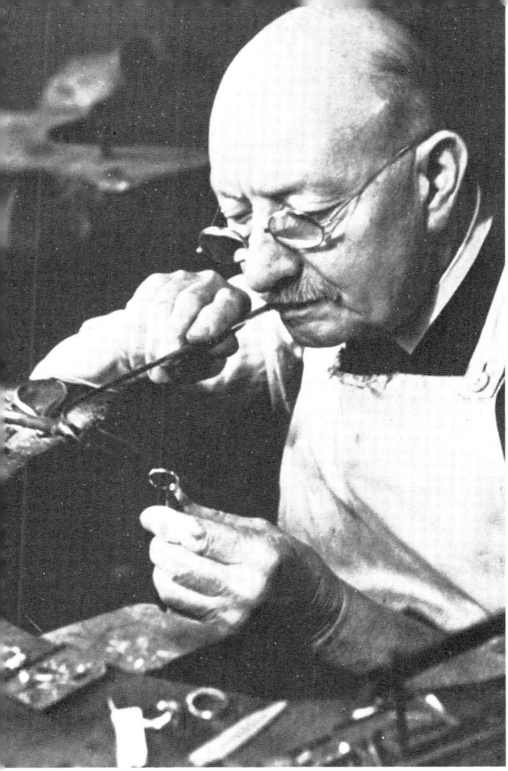

▲ A craftsman from Birmingham using a mouth blow pipe and gas flame in exactly the same way as the ancient Egyptians used a reed with a clay nozzle and an open flame.

◀ The workshop of a modern exclusive jewellers. Each piece produced is designed by one of the house designers, then hand-made by a highly-skilled craftsman.

a mass-production workshop, from a hand-made workshop, or from the workshop of an artist-craftsman. Generally mass production articles are sold in high street jewellers, hand-made articles are available from exclusive jewellery houses, and the work of the artist-craftsman goes either directly to the client who has commissioned the piece, or to a craft shop or boutique.

In the mass production of jewellery, thousands of identical articles are shaped by large presses or stamping machines.

When it is necessary to join parts together, the jewellery is soldered either by a craftsman, or with small electric arc welding machines. Jigs hold correctly the sections to be joined. The operators place the pieces in the jigs, turn on the machines, check the pieces are soldered, then move on to the next identical piece.

Jewellery can also be cast. A craftsman is needed to make the original pattern, but after that all stages can be produced en masse by specialist machinery.

It is usual to tumble-polish such mass produced articles rather than polish by hand. In the tumble-polishing process all pieces are loaded into barrels with assorted polished steel shot and a lubricant. The barrels are rotated until the work is polished. This process is similar to a pebble being polished as it rolls around on a sandy beach.

The designs for mass produced jewellery are limited by the capabilities of the machines, and the sales prospects of the piece. It would be uneconomical to set up machinery to produce jewellery of limited appeal.

Hand-made jewellery

The exclusive jewellery houses operate workshops in which the majority of pieces are hand-made. Some will go into the stock of the retail outlet of the workshop. Other pieces will have been specifically commissioned by clients and will be made to their particular requirements. Workshops such as these normally produce jewellery of the highest quality only.

The artist-craftsman will normally produce jewellery in any price range. His concern is primarily with the excellence of the design, and he is likely to combine the materials and techniques of many disciplines to achieve his aim.

Design your jewellery

Designing is a continuous process of observation and selection. The designer of jewellery selects shapes and lines, interprets these in a suitable material, then arranges the lines, shapes and material into a wearable form. Choose a stimulus. It can be a natural shape, a manufactured object, or a spontaneous idea. Work with a pencil, paints, or modelling materials such as cardboard and plasticine and, by changing the relationships between areas or lines, investigate the idea. When researching, look at the contrasts between shapes and lines, the direction, width and implied area of the lines and consider the balance and the surface treatment.

▲ To design a round pendant, one way is to select the appealing lines from a chosen stimulus, in this case a flower. Next, choose shapes and lines and arrange these within the circle. The end result does not necessarily resemble the stimulus.

▼ Both the line and shape of the building are appealing. Sketch the building. Draw it from different angles, then select and rearrange lines and shapes. Do not preconceive the jewellery, but allow the progress of the sketches to suggest ideas.

▶ The paintings and jewellery made up from the final design. The stimulus is a point from which to start and should not be a restriction. The pendant no longer looks like a flower, but the ring retains some of the qualities of the building.

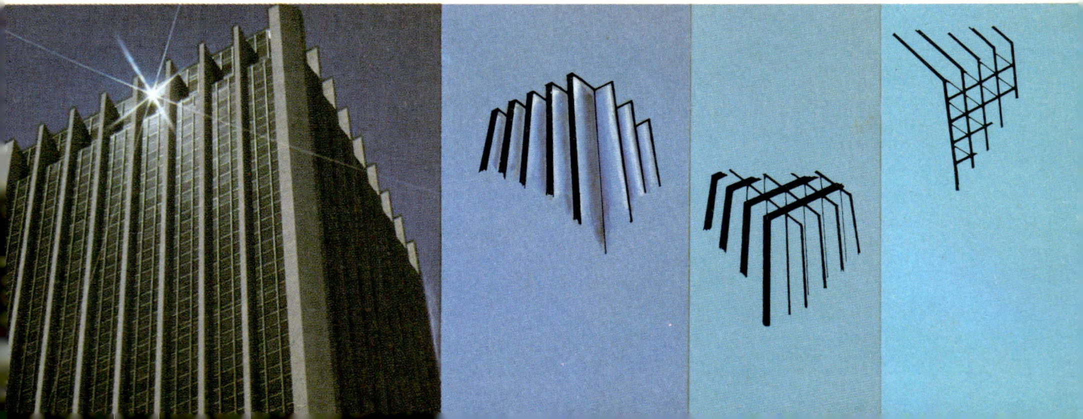

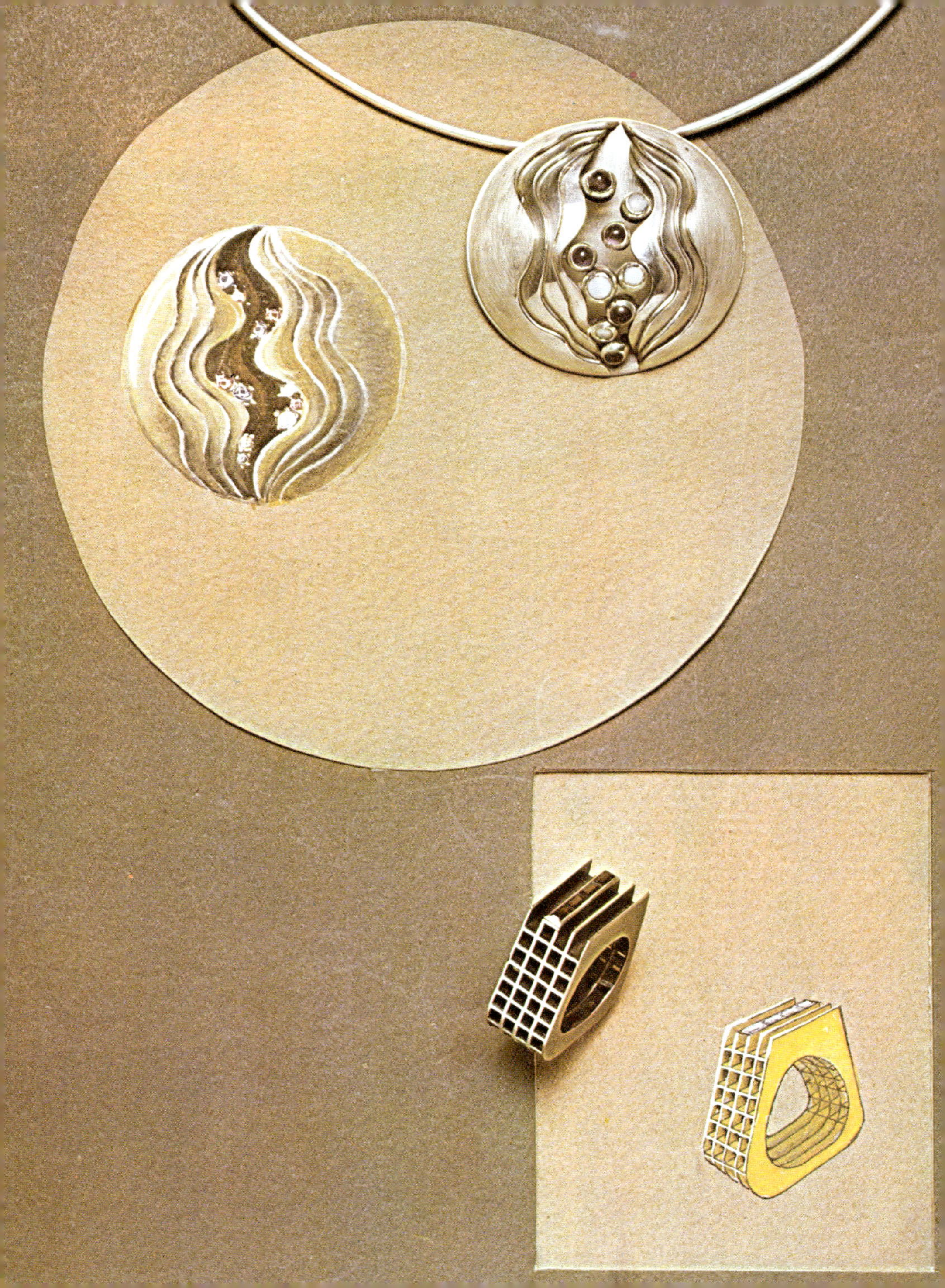

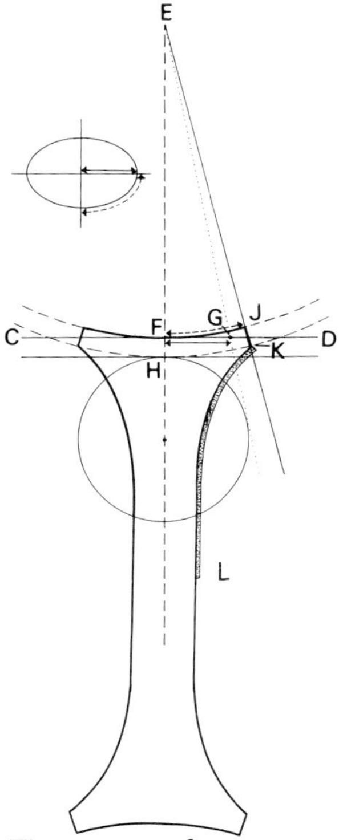

The pattern for a cone

Cones are often used to set tumbled stones. Make the pattern in the following way.

Mark the diameter of the base and the height of the cone. With the centre of the compass at A draw an arc to pass through B and C. The circumference of the base of the cone is equal to its diameter multiplied by π (about 22/7), so mark off this length on the arc. The pattern is as shown below.

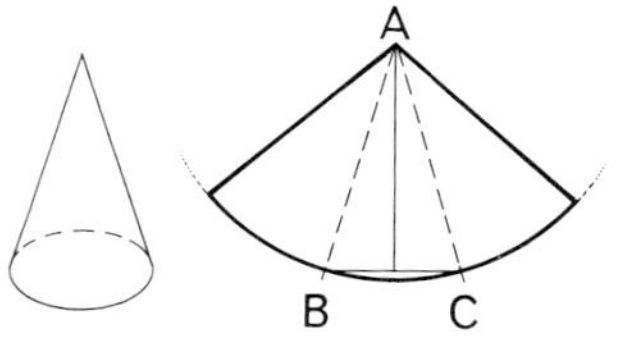

Constructing patterns

To make the pattern for a hollow ring (see p. 78), follow the steps set out below.

Measure the finger and draw a circle the size of the ring. Draw a tangent to the circle at H. Draw a line CD parallel to this tangent to represent the position of the base of the stone above the finger. Draw a line through the centre of the circle and perpendicular to CD at F. Mark G on CD so that FG is equal to half the width of the stone. Draw a tangent to the circle passing through G to cut the perpendicular line at E. With the centre at E, draw arcs as shown through F and H. Mark off FJ equal to a quarter of the circumference of the stone and join EJ.

Cut a length of wire equal to half the circumference of the finger size. Bend it to form the curve KL, taking into account the width of the finger band required. This construction forms a quarter of the pattern. Now use carbon paper to transfer this to the other three quarters.

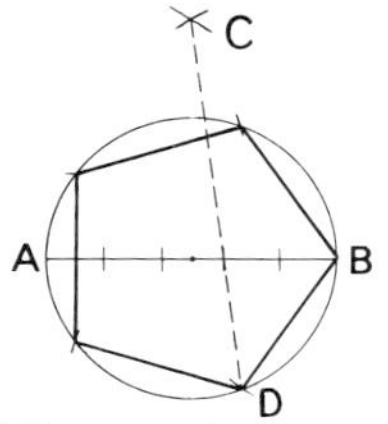

Dividing a circle

It is often necessary to divide a circle into a number of equal parts. This is the method to use.

Draw in the diameter AB of the circle. Open the compass to the length AB, and with firstly A, then B, draw arcs to cross at C. Now divide the line AB into the number of parts required, in this case five. Draw a line from C through the second point from B, to cross the circle at D. Measure the distance from D to B with a compass, and mark this length around the circle as shown above. The circle will now be divided into five equal parts.

Oval

Many stones are oval, so this is a shape which occurs frequently in jewellery.

To construct an oval, draw two lines at right angles and mark off the length and width of the oval required. This is shown in the diagram below. Mark a point N on MO so that MN = OP. Lay the straight edge of a piece of paper along MO and mark the points M′, N′, and O′ on the paper. Now gradually slide the point O′ down the line from O to P, making sure that the point N′ moves along the line from N to O. Mark several positions of M′. The positions of the paper are shown by the dotted lines on the diagram. Join all the M′ points to form a quarter of the oval. Transfer this quarter to complete the pattern.

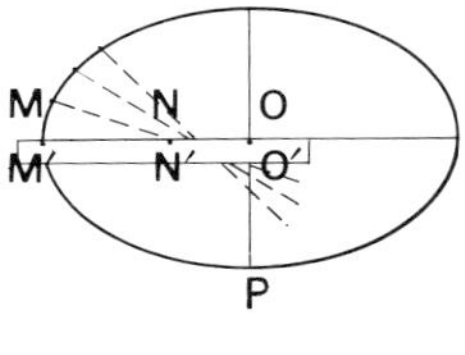

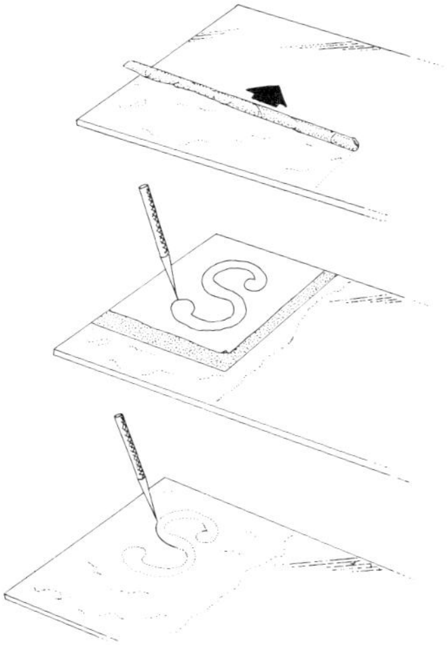

▲ Stages of transferring a design using carbon paper.

Transferring designs

Having designed a piece of jewellery, the next stage is to transfer the pattern to the material. If the design is flat, or has only slight bends in it, the pattern can be transferred directly. But if the design includes metal that curves back on itself, then a different technique is needed.

Transferring simple designs

One method involves the use of carbon paper.

First, make the surface of the metal dirty by rolling plasticine over it. This is necessary because carbon paper does not mark clean, shiny silver. Lay carbon paper over the metal, place the design on the carbon paper and, with a scriber, trace the outline of the pattern. This leaves a fine black line which rubs off easily. Mark along the carbon line with a scriber to scratch the design into the metal.

Designs can also be transferred using clear acetate. This technique is used by engravers because it is suited to transferring fine lines, and the pattern ends up in reverse. Since either side of the metal can be used this will not usually matter.

The first step is to place the acetate over the design and scratch the outline into the acetate. With a sharp blade, powder some pencil lead onto the scratched surface. Rub a finger over the acetate to push the lead into the grooves, then clean off the excess.

Roll plasticine over the metal, lay the acetate, scratch side down, in place and secure it. Burnish the outline onto the metal by rubbing with any suitable smooth surface. Scribe along the fine black line to mark the design into the metal.

▼ Stages of transferring a design using acetate.

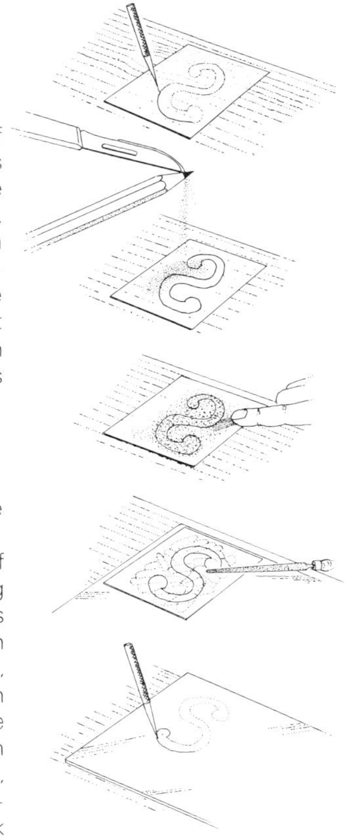

To make a scriber

Grind a point onto any steel rod about 4 mm in diameter. Make the point fine and sharp for acetate and metal, and slightly rounded for carbon paper.

Patterns for twists

When the design includes shapes that turn back or twist as shown, the pattern for transferring has to be traced in a different way.

Begin by drawing a tangent on the design at the start of the twist. Next, on tracing paper, trace the pattern up to the tangent, and trace in the tangent. Lift the tracing paper from the design, turn the tracing paper over, and replace it, realigning the tangents. Trace the remainder of the outline. Both parts of the pattern can be seen through the tracing paper. Transfer the complete shape to the metal in the normal way.

To work

Jewellery can be designed and made with very few tools. A piercing saw, a couple of pairs of pliers with smooth jaws, some files, a hammer and a small blow torch are adequate for learning the first stages. These tools are readily available and take up very little space. A board to cover the kitchen table provides an adequate working surface, and a bench pin to lean the work against can be attached to the board. The whole working area can be held secure with G-clamps, and removed when the table is again required. The blow torch flame is small and easy to use and most pieces of jewellery can be soldered on a charcoal block resting on the table.

▲ Working at the kitchen table.

Sitting position

A jeweller's bench is usually about 90 cm high. The height of the stool is adjusted to allow full view of the work and a comfortable sawing position. Normally, at the correct position, the elbows can rest on the bench just below shoulder level.

Kitchen tables are about 75 cm high, so either raise the table or lower the stool to get the right position.

Bench pin

A bench pin is a wooden wedge that can be cut or filed to give the best support for any particular piece. Some craftsmen file on the sloping side, others work on the level side and saw off a small slanting face. Sometimes a key-hole shape is cut into the pin to help while sawing.

Costing

The cost of the metal for a job can be calculated from the table on p. 87 if the following are known:

1. Thickness of metal in mm.
2. Area of metal in sq cm.
3. Cost per gramme of metal.

If the design fits into a rectangle of 7 cm x 2 cm, then the area is 14 sq cm. If the metal is 1.5 mm thick, from the table it is found that for silver of this thickness, every sq cm weighs 1.56 grammes. So the weight of metal is 14 x 1.56 gm, that is, 21.84 gm. Multiply this figure by the cost per gramme to get the total cost of the metal.

To calculate the cost of reproducing a piece in another metal, refer to p. 87.

Always save any scraps or filings of previous metal. Remelt whole pieces to re-use the metal and resell filings (lemmel) to the dealer. Filings contain small particles of iron which will cause cracking in the metal if they are melted with the whole pieces.

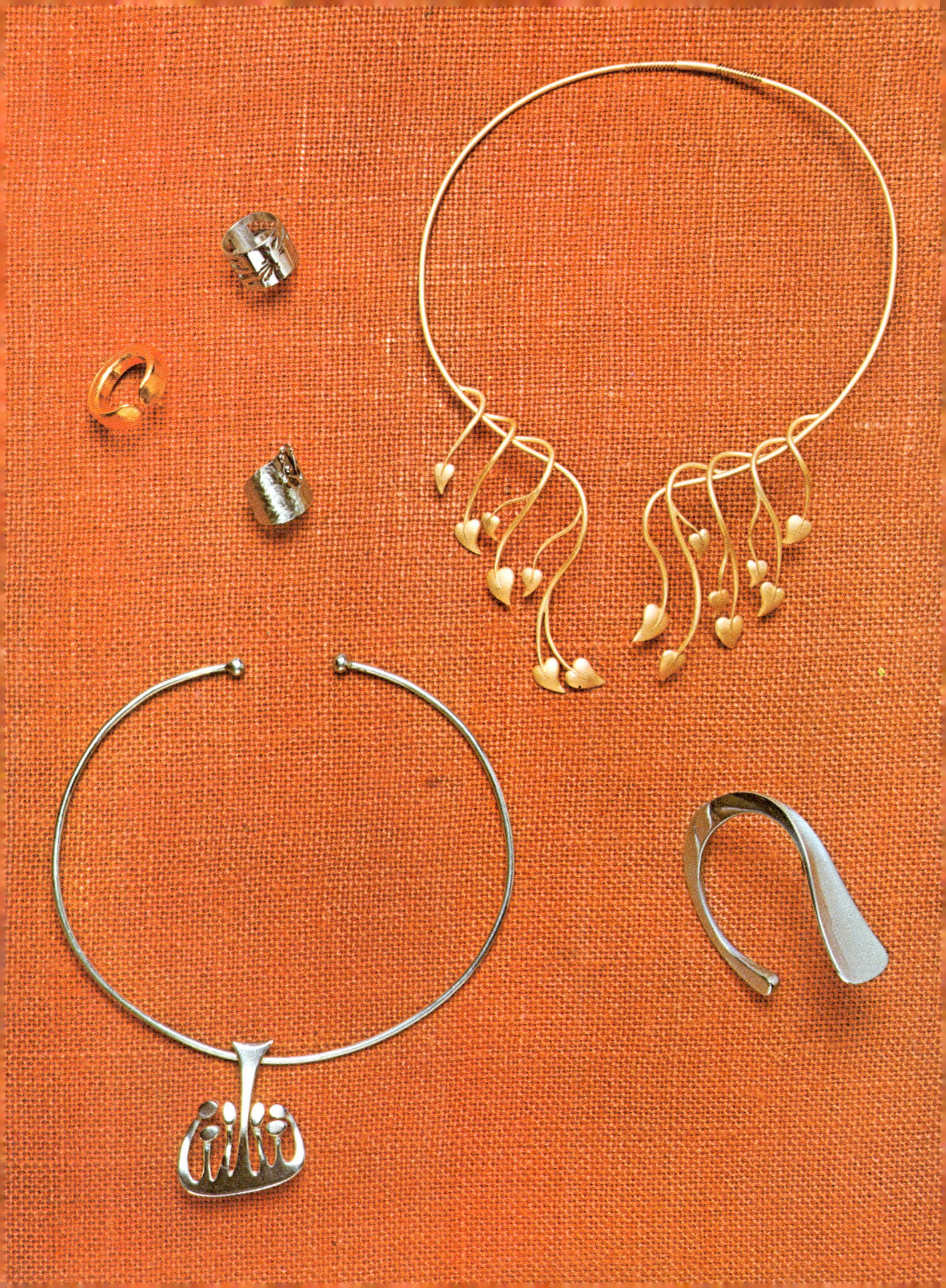

Basic processes

The metals traditionally used for jewellery are chosen for their beauty, durability, and workability. Polished or unpolished gold and silver have a pleasing colour. These metals are not subject to normal corrosion, and they are easily cut and manipulated. The basic processes of sawing, filing, drilling and shaping metals are quickly mastered. To begin, design some simple articles that require these techniques and start making original jewellery while learning the initial steps. After that, try more advanced pieces using the same techniques. Tools that feel strange at first become more comfortable to use.

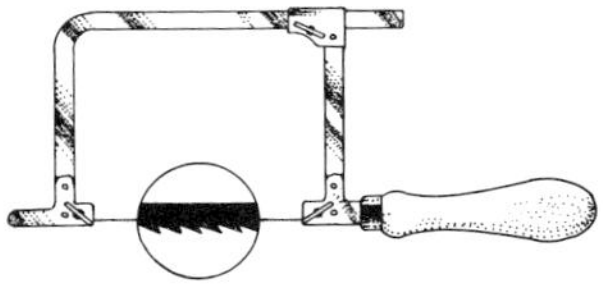

▲ An adjustable piercing saw. Non-adjustable frames are also available.

Sawing

Jewellers use the piercing saw for cutting metal. The saw blade normally used is size 2/0. It is about 130 x 0.2 x 0.5 mm. Finer blades, 3/0 to very fine 8/0, are for delicate work. Occasionally, coarser blades (1/0, 0, 1) are needed. The blade is held under tension in a piercing saw frame. The teeth face towards the handle.

To secure the blade, insert one end into the frame and tighten the wing nut. Push the top of the frame against the bench and, with the frame bent, secure the other end of the blade. The blade should "ping" when plucked. The correct tension is important; a slack blade will jam and break and a blade that is too taut may break before it is used.

To saw

Lubricate the blade with beeswax. Hold the metal firmly on the bench pin. To begin, draw the corner of the blade across the metal. Straighten the frame and, with the frame upright, saw with long even strokes. The downward strokes are the cutting strokes. Use the full length of the blade, and allow the weight of the frame to do the work.

Turn corners by moving the blade up and down in the same place, gradually turning the frame until the blade is facing in the new direction.

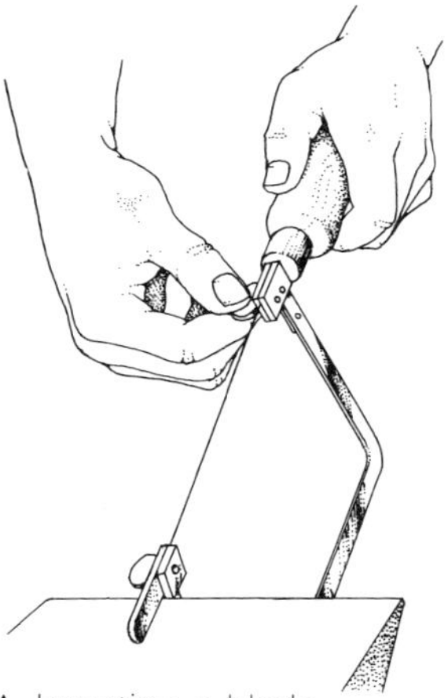

▲ Inserting a blade.

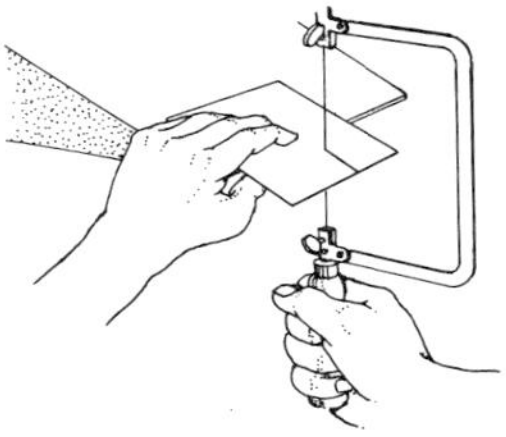

▲ Normal upright sawing position.

Use the edge of the blade as a file to ease off small inaccuracies. With the top of the saw frame slanting slightly forward, use the corner of the blade to cut precise and sharp detail.

To pierce out an enclosed area, drill a small hole, pass a saw blade through, then fix it in the frame and saw.

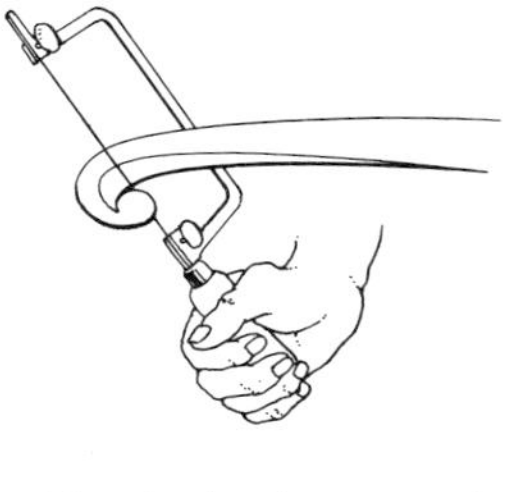

▲ Position for intricate work.

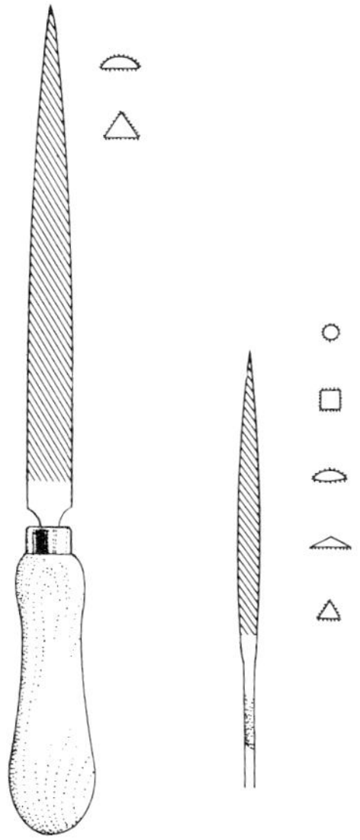

▲ Hand and needle files.

Filing

Filing gradually reduces material to the required shape and size.

Tools

Useful hand files are a three-square and a half-round, both 20 cm long and No. 2 cut. These require handles. Needle files are about 12 cm long. Suitable types are round, square, sage-leaf, safety-back, and three-square.

To file

Hold the work steady by bracing it against the bench pin. For accurate filing, choose the largest file for the piece being made. Lay the file diagonally across the surface and file with long, even strokes. Keep the file in contact with the work all the time. The forward stroke is the cutting stroke and requires slightly greater pressure. For curves, choose a file that suits the shape.

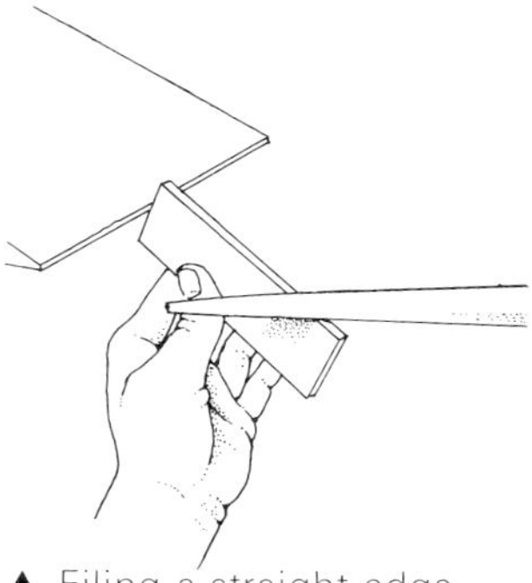

▲ Filing a straight edge.

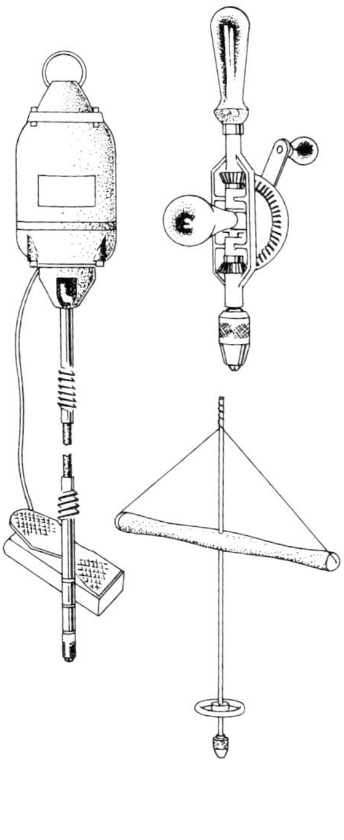

Drilling

Suitable drills are a pendant drill (a suspended electric drill with a flexible shaft), a hand drill, and a bow drill. The hand and electric drills take standard twist drills. For a bow drill, a drill is made from a needle to cut in both directions. The advantage of a bow drill is that it is used with one hand.

To drill with a bow drill

Twist the top to wind the string around the shaft. With two fingers each side of the handle, push down. As the drill turns, allow the handle to rise back up the shaft. Push down again. This knack is soon acquired.

◀ Pendant, hand, and bow drills.

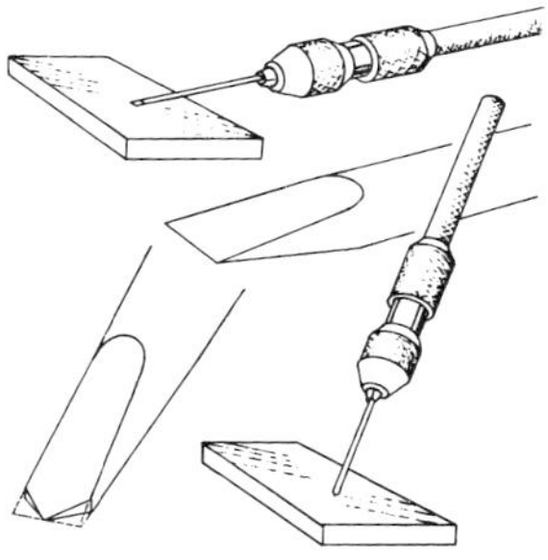

▲ The faces on a needle drill.

To make a needle drill

With two pairs of pliers, snap a needle in half. Hold one piece in a pin vice with the broken end protruding. On a rub-stone lubricated with a little oil, rub down the two long flat faces. Then rub off the corners of the wedge to form the two cutting faces.

Bending metal

Sheet metal or wire can be bent with pliers. The metal should normally be annealed first (see page 41).

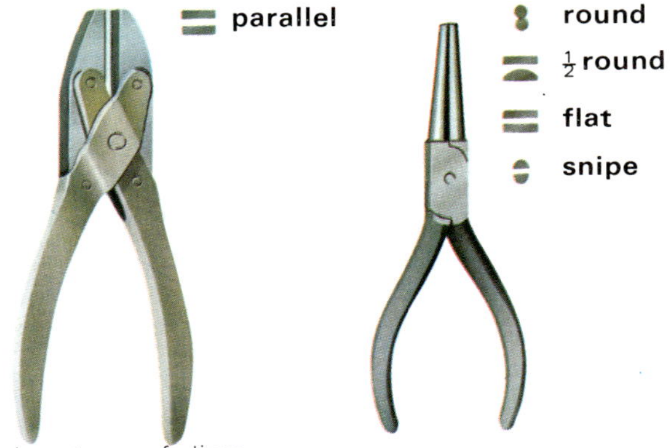

▲ Various types of pliers.

Tools

The jaws of pliers should be smooth and polished. Serrated jaws will put marks in metal and these are often difficult to remove.

Some uses of pliers:
round-nose pliers are used for bending small rings or tight curves;
flat-nose pliers are for straightening kinks or bending right angles;
half-round pliers are for turning up rings (the half-round jaw is used on the inside of the curve so that the metal is not damaged);
snipe-nose pliers are for adjusting jump rings or working in difficult places;
parallel pliers are used to hold metal while working (the metal is secure because the jaws grip along their whole length).

To bend metal

For a finger ring, use half-round pliers. Bend each end of the metal to the required curve. Then, moving the pliers along the metal a few millimetres at a time, bend the rest of the metal to follow the curve.

For a flat ring, experiment to find the maximum thickness and width of metal strip that can be bent. This depends on the strength of the individual. About one-third of the way down the jaws of half-round pliers, file opposing grooves about 1 mm deep with a three-square needle file. Hold the strip in a pair of flat-nose pliers so that, as pressure is applied with the half-round pliers, the strip locks against the base of the jaws. Grip the strip in the filed groove of the half-round pliers, and start to pull the metal into a flat ring. Anneal and continue bending.

Sometimes two pairs of pliers are necessary to twist or shape metal.

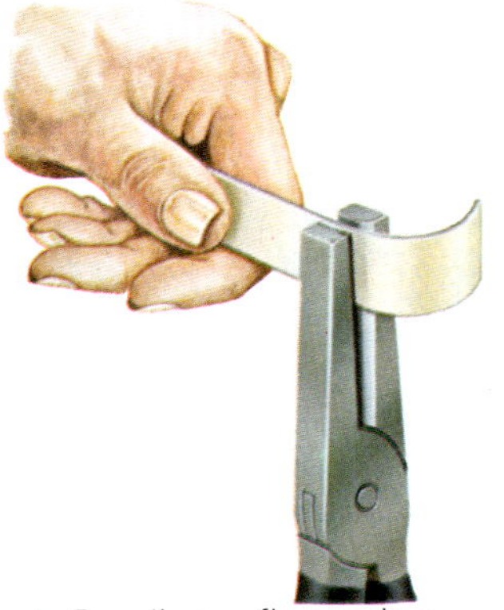

▲ Bending a finger ring.

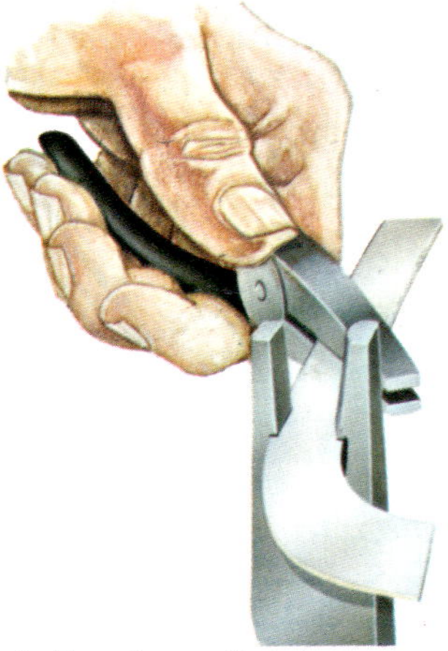

▲ Bending a flat ring.

▲ Using two pairs of pliers.

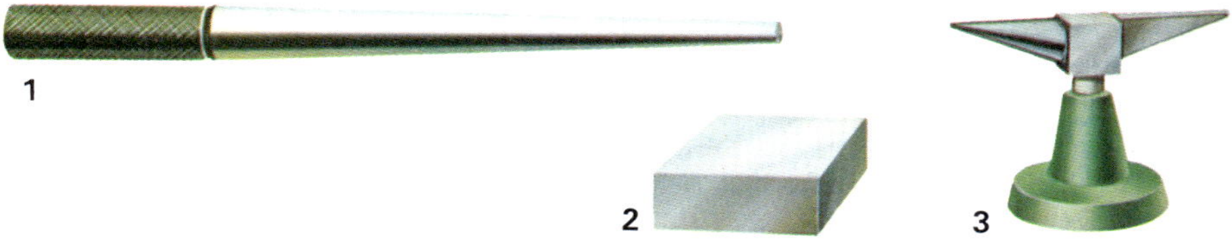

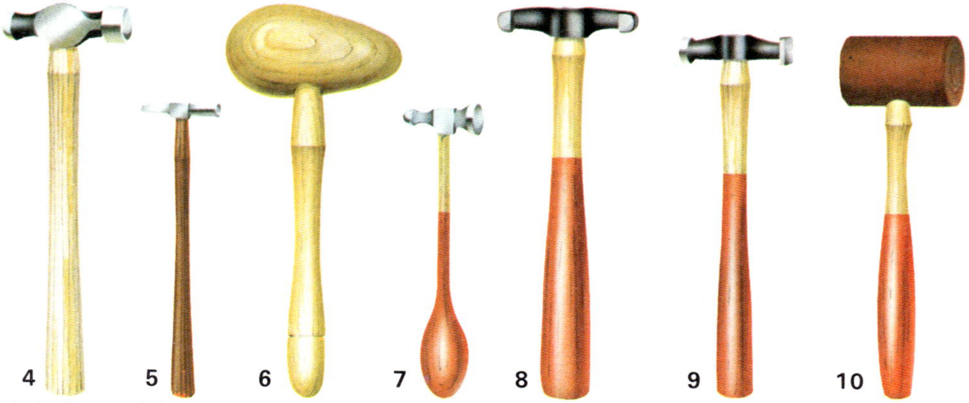

▲ **1.** Steel triplet.
2. Flat steel block
3. Steel anvil.

4. Ball pien hammer
5. Cross pien or jeweller's hammer.

6. Wooden mallet.
7. Chasing hammer.
8. Raising hammer.
9. Planishing hammer.
10. Hide mallet.

Forming metals

Metal can be stretched, compressed and reshaped with hammers. Frequent annealing is required in the shaping process (see page 41).

Tools

Wooden and hide mallets shape metal without greatly marking it. To reshape or stretch metal, hit it with a steel hammer onto a steel anvil, steel block, or steel triblet. Tap weak or thin sections with a small jeweller's hammer.

Hit punches with a chasing hammer. The broad face is designed to allow the craftsman to attend to the piece of work and not be concerned with watching that the hammer hits the punch. The ball end of the handle is pivoted in the hand so that the hammer head bounces on the punch. This ensures even taps.

The ball end of a ball pien hammer head extends metal; the flat end is for general hammering. Hitting with the nose of the raising hammer head compresses metal, while hammering with the flat of the face extends the metal. The direction in which the metal is extended most is the direction parallel to the handle as the hammer hits. Marks made in the metal by the raising hammer are removed by gentle, even tapping with the planishing hammer.

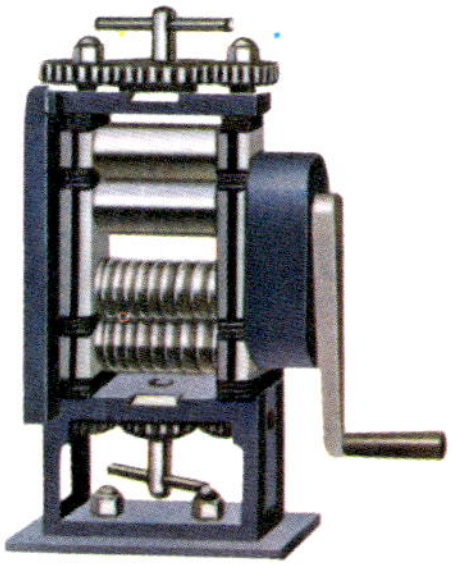

▲ Steel rolling mills will thin metal, and extend it mainly in the direction in which the metal is fed between the rollers. The mills have adjustable rollers for sheet and wire. Most college workshops have mills but they are generally considered to be too expensive for home use.

Shaping metal

Precious metals can be punched into almost any shape. A doming block with graded semi-spherical holes is for punching a flat disc into a dome. A swage block is for shaping a strip of metal into a U-section. A leather bag filled with sand supports larger areas of metal being initially shaped. A lead cake (a block of lead) or a pitch block is suitable for supporting metal when forming high relief. The lead gives beneath the blow of the punch while still holding up the surrounding metal. Lead contaminates precious metals, so always work with a sheet of paper over the lead.

Metal being shaped should be kept well annealed. (See p. 41.)

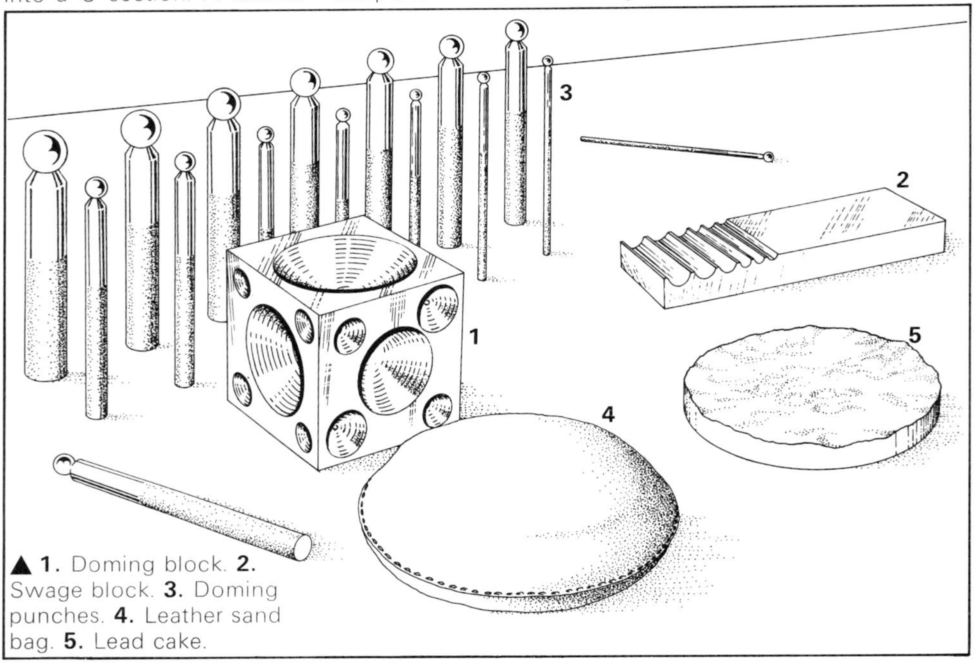

▲ **1.** Doming block. **2.** Swage block. **3.** Doming punches. **4.** Leather sand bag. **5.** Lead cake.

To forge a ring

▼ Anneal a silver bar 30 mm x 5 mm x 5 mm.

▼ Flatten the ends by hitting them with a raising hammer on a steel stake.

▼ Anneal, then dish the flattened areas with the ball end of a ball pien hammer.

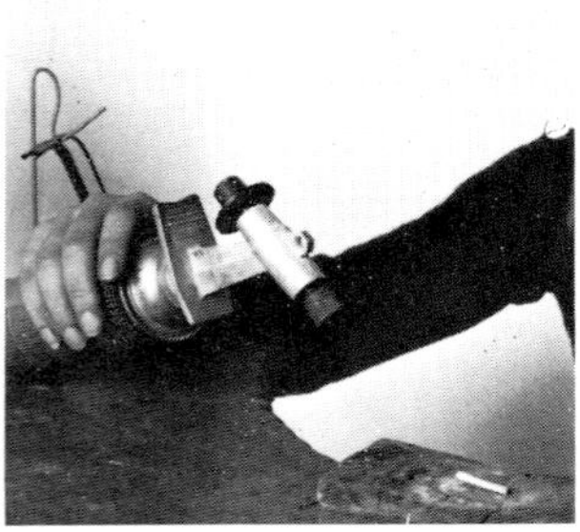

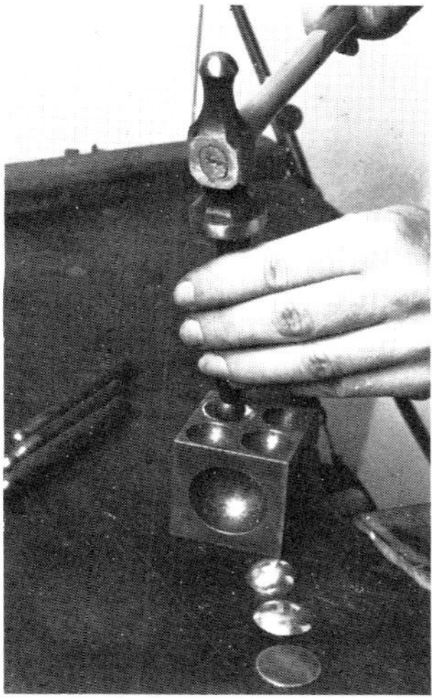

▲ To dome a metal disc, begin with the largest punch and the largest hole. The disc should not overlap the hole. Tap the punch onto the disc, keeping the punch moving over the metal so as to shape the metal evenly. Work down the graded holes to the required size.

▼ To U-shape a metal strip, lay the strip in the largest groove of the swage block. The strip should not be wider than the groove. Hit the side of a doming punch onto the strip to push it into the groove. To avoid damaging the punch use a wooden mallet. Begin with the largest groove and work down the series of grooves until the desired shape is achieved.

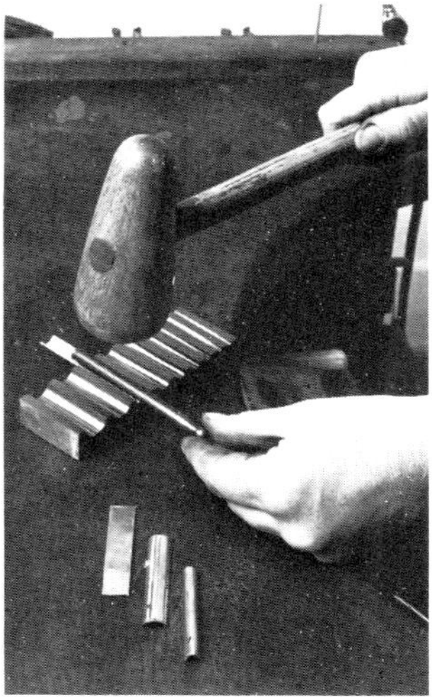

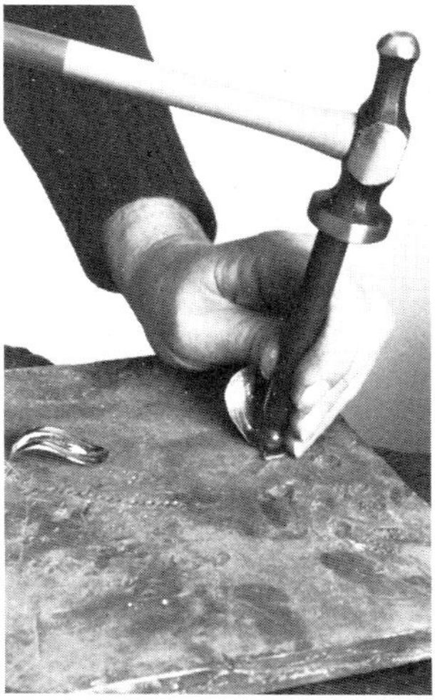

▲ To punch out a relief design, use a lead cake. Resting the little finger on the lead as a guide, move the punch over the work while repeatedly bouncing the hammer head on the punch. The even blows will ensure a smooth depression.

▼ Anneal before shaping the ring with a wooden mallet on a steel triblet.

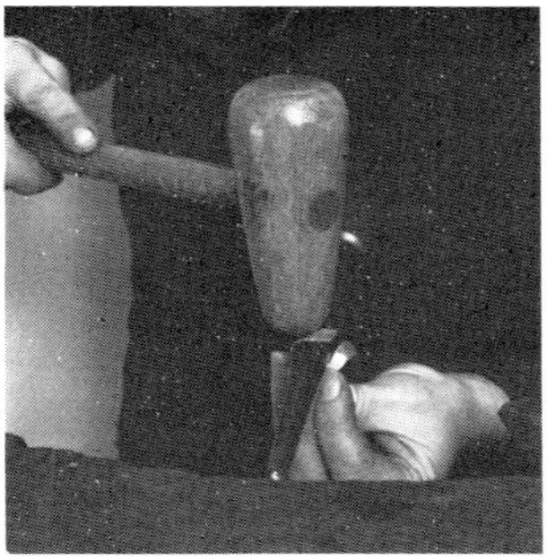

▼ File off hammer marks. Sandpaper away file marks, then polish.

▼ The finished piece. Forging gives a change in contour and thickness.

The use of heat

In jewellery-making, heat is used to soften metal, to join it, and to melt it. When precious metal is deformed, as by hammering or bending, it tends to become hard and springy. This is known as work hardening. To make the metal easily workable again, it is heated to a dull red colour. This is called annealing. Metal is joined with solder in a process known as hard soldering. The join is prepared, solder applied, and the job heated. When the temperature reaches the melting point of the solder, it flows to make the join. To melt metal, heat is applied until first the surface, then the whole mass becomes molten.

Sources of heat

The heat sources suitable for jewellery work are numerous. There are mains gas-air blow torches, torches using gas from a pressurised container, or a mouth blow pipe to direct an open flame.

The small torch with a hand-held gas cylinder is both cheap and good. The larger bottle-gas torch has interchangeable nozzles giving a wide variation in flame size.

If mains gas is available, the small mouth blow torch is useful. For larger work, the torch burning a mixture of mains gas and compressed air is necessary.

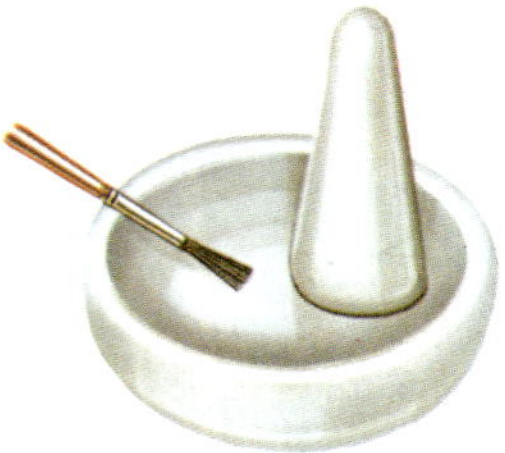

▲ A borax cone, dish, and borax brush.

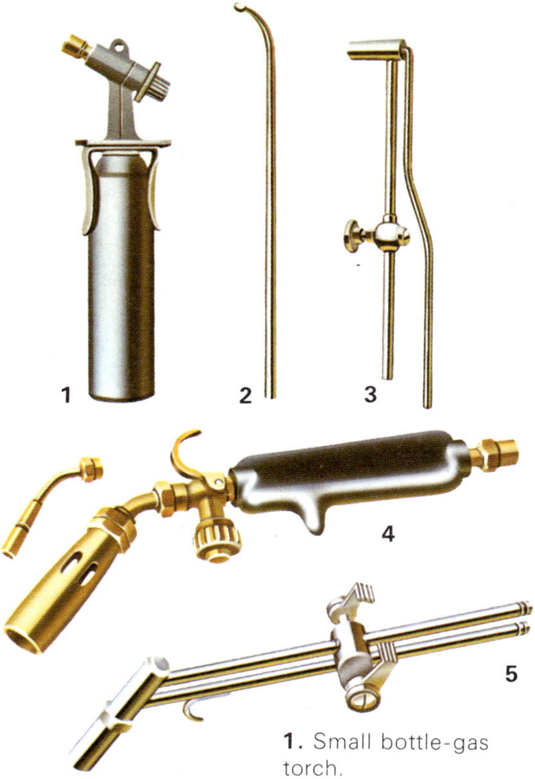

1. Small bottle-gas torch.
2. Mouth blowpipe.
3. Mouth blow torch.
4. Large bottle-gas torch.
5. Compressed air torch.

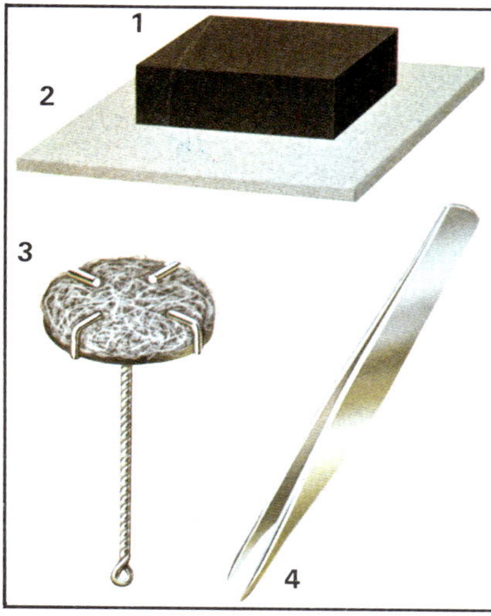

▲ A soft flame or reducing flame.

▲ A hard flame or oxidizing flame.

◀ **1.** Charcoal block. **2.** Synthetic soldering block. **3.** Soldering wig. **4.** Tweezers.

Flames

The size and heat of a flame depends on the mixture of gas and air. The hottest part of the flame is just ahead of the light blue point.

A soft flame is suitable for annealing and for most soldering jobs, as a whole area can be heated uniformly. A hard flame is not often used because of the risk of overheating and melting the metal in one spot. Even for small soldering jobs, such as joining the links of a chain, it is better to use a small soft flame.

What to heat on

To heat the work, rest it on a synthetic soldering block, a charcoal block, or a wire wig. A charcoal block retains heat. It sometimes smoulders and should be quenched (dipped in water) after use to stop continued burning. A wig allows heat to circulate around the metal.

Melting metal

Coat solder-free metal with flux to prevent oxidization and place it either in a crucible or in a hollow, carved in a charcoal block. Using a large, soft flame, heat until all the metal is molten and the surface "rolls". Allow the ball of metal to cool, then pickle.

When working with molten metal, take great care to avoid accidents.

Annealing metal

Whenever metal becomes work-hardened it can be resoftened by annealing. To do this, play a large, soft flame evenly over the metal until it is dull red. The colour is difficult to see in bright light so turn the table light off.

After heating, cool the metal by either leaving it on a steel block or holding it under water. Clean it by pickling.

Anneal wire in a coil, or direct a flame along the wire while holding it in steel tweezers.

Pickle

Flux and oxides formed on metal during heating are cleaned off with pickle. Suitable pickles are warmed dilute sulphuric acid (1 part acid, 9 parts water), alum crystals dissolved in simmering water, or one of the patent safety pickles.

Handle acid with extreme care and keep it out of the reach of children and animals. When mixing acid, always add acid to water to avoid overheating and possible explosion. Store in a labelled, glass-stoppered bottle.

Wash the piece in water after pickling.

If acid seeps into inaccessible places, boil the work in washing soda and water to neutralize the acid.

Hard solder

For the hard soldering process on jewellery, the solder used is an alloy of lower melting point than the metal to be joined and is matched to the metal. For example, silver solder is used for joining silver, and 18 ct yellow gold solder for 18 ct yellow gold.

Some pieces require many soldering stages. If all solder melted at the same temperature, the later heatings might melt the solder in the earlier joints, causing the pieces to move. So, solders with different melting temperatures are used.

These grades of solder are enamelling, hard, medium, and easy. Enamelling has the highest melting point and is normally used only for work to be enamelled. Usually, the first solderings on a piece are made with hard solder which melts at the second highest temperature. Medium is used next, then easy. Several joins can be made with each grade before a lower one is needed.

Solder flows by capillary action between two closely fitting, clean surfaces. It does not bridge gaps, or fill holes, so careful preparation of a join is needed for successful soldering.

Silver and gold solder is made in thin sheets or sticks. Jewellers cut solder with shears into pieces about 0.5 mm thick and 1 mm square. These small snippets, called pallions, are positioned every 2 to 3 mm along a join and are carefully placed to touch both sides.

Soft solder

Soft solder contains lead and tin. It will join precious metals, but is inappropriate for jewellery as the colour is dull grey. Also, soft-soldered jobs cannot be hall-marked because lead and tin fall below the standards required for precious metals.

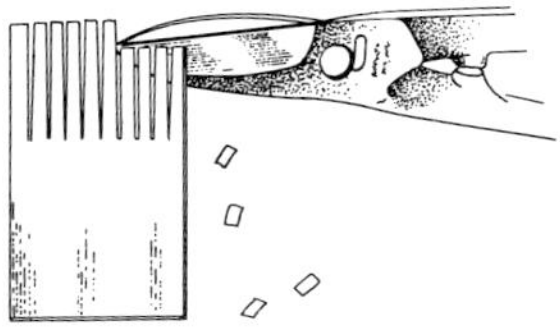

▲ Snip the solder into a fringe. Cut off pallions as needed into a small container.

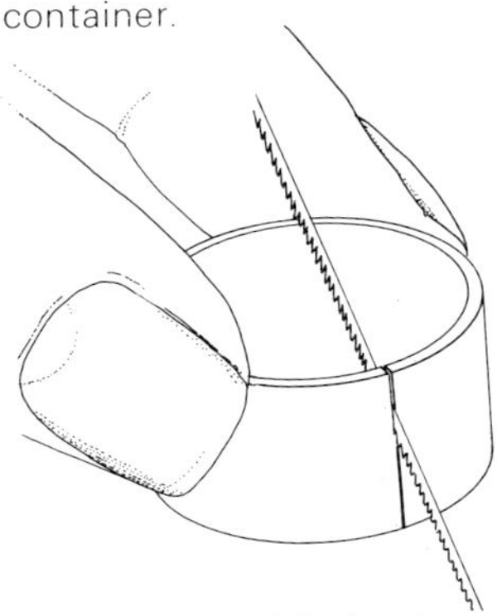

▲ Prepare the join in a finger ring by pressing the sides of the ring and sawing down the crack between the ends. Several such sawings will remove any high spots. Alternatively, file the ends.

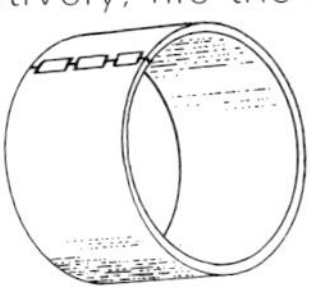

▲ Place pallions of solder running along the join and touching both sides of it.

Flux

During heating, oxide forms on the surface of metal. This inhibits the flow of solder. So for soldering, both the solder and the metal surfaces are kept free of oxide by coating with flux. Borax is the flux normally used by jewellers, although various commercial fluxes are available.

Flux is applied with a small, soft-haired watercolour brush.

Preparation for hard soldering

Saw or file the surfaces to be joined until they butt together tightly and evenly. Apply flux where the solder is required to flow. Place pallions of solder in position with a borax brush.

To solder

Begin heating gently with a soft flame. Watch the piece and do not overheat the metal.

First, water will evaporate from the borax causing it to bubble, or "flower". The pallions may move. If they do not settle back into the right place as heating continues, remove the flame and replace them. With further heating, the borax darkens and then the solder flows. When the bright, silver line of the molten solder appears along the join, stop heating immediately. Cool the work on a steel block or quench it in water.

Finally, check the soldering, then pickle to remove the oxide and flux.

1

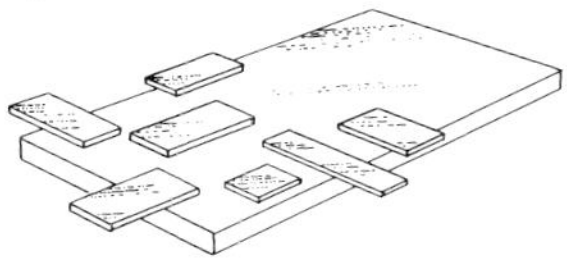

2

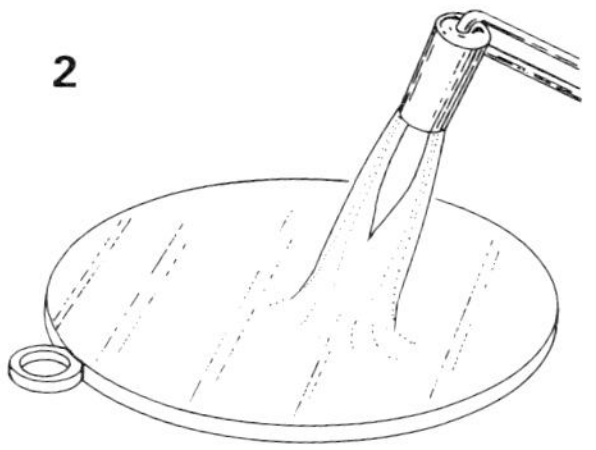

3

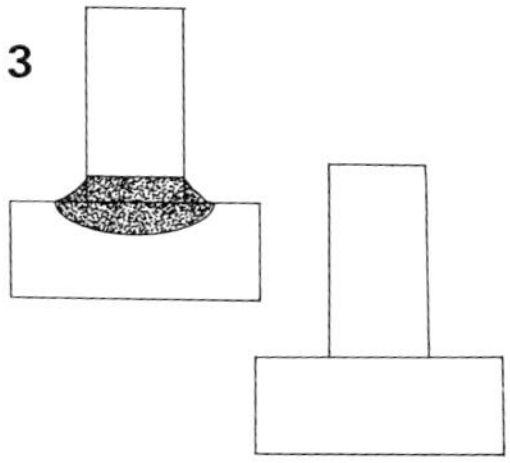

4

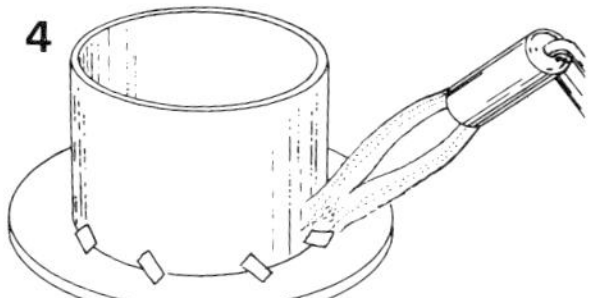

5

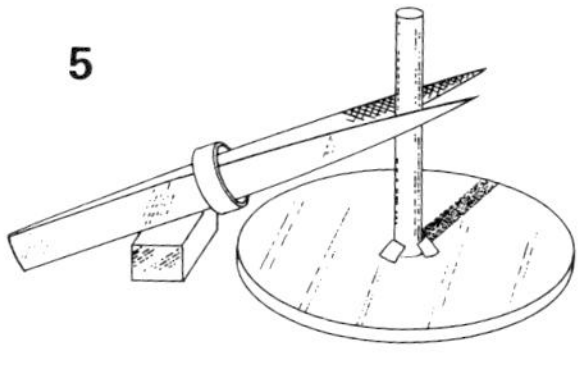

6

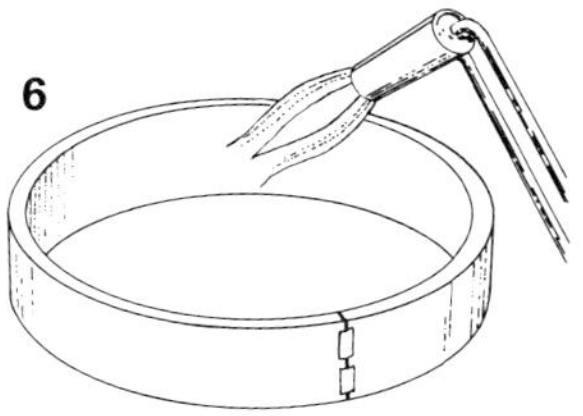

1. Multi-stage soldering
Ensure that the surfaces to be soldered fit tightly and are clean. Cut only sufficient pallions of hard solder for the initial solderings. Flux the surfaces, position the pallions, and solder the join. Usually, hard solder can be used on three or four joins before a lower grade is needed.

If flux still covers the surface, arrange the next parts of the piece and solder with medium. But if the surface has a dark oxide coating, pickle, wash thoroughly under water, then reflux and solder.

After three or four joins with medium solder, prepare the work for the next soldering stage. Finish the piece with easy solder. Cool and pickle.

2. Soldering small sections of metal to larger ones
Solder will flow between two surfaces of metal when they are both hot enough. When a small piece of metal is to be soldered onto a larger one, the heat should be directed onto the larger area. For instance, when soldering a small hanging ring to a pendant, direct the flame onto the pendant. Heat will flow to the ring.

If the flame is played onto the ring, it will heat rapidly. Solder will flow onto the ring as soon as it reaches the melting point of the solder, but the solder will not flow onto the cooler pendant. So the ring will not be joined to the pendant.

3. How much solder?
Usually small pallions every 2 to 3 mm along a join will be sufficient. Do not overload the solder. It should fill the seam, but should not be built up around the join.

4. Positioning the work for soldering
Where possible, position the parts of the work so that gravity holds the metal in place during soldering.

If a piece of metal moves while heating, use a pair of steel tweezers to replace it quickly without withdrawing the flame.

5. Supporting the work while soldering
Sometimes a part of the work cannot easily be balanced for soldering. A wire loop slid down around tweezers will keep them shut. They can then be used to clamp a piece of metal in place during soldering.

6. Direction of heat
Metal under tension may spring apart during heating. For instance, metal that has just been hammered around a triblet to form a ring is work-hardened and springy. If heat is applied to the join only, the opposite side, acting as a spring, will open the join. To prevent this happening, heat the middle of the metal strip first. This effectively anneals the metal, and the seam will remain shut. Gradually bring the heat to the join.

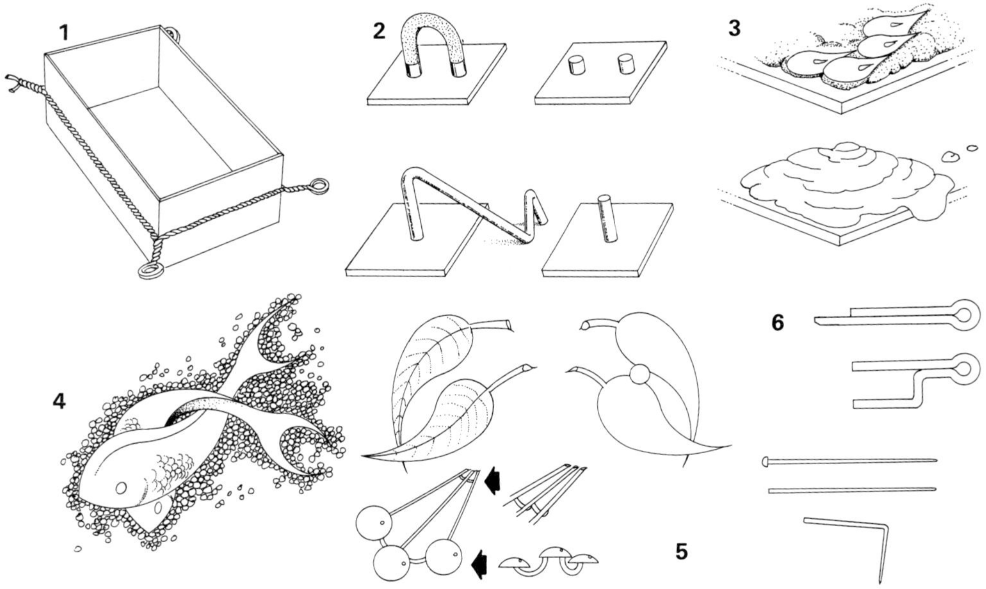

Hints for soldering

1. Steel wire, called binding wire (0.2 to 0.3 mm thick), can be used to tie pieces of metal together to prevent their moving during soldering. Bind the work with two strands of the wire twisted together. This increases its strength and allows for expansion.

A tight wire around a corner will cut. To prevent this, twist a loop at the corner. To tighten the wire around the job, twist the ends together. Steel wire would contaminate the pickle, so remove it before pickling.

2. To solder two adjacent pegs, first bend up a U-shaped wire. It will stand by itself if the ends are filed flat. Balance the U-shape on the piece and solder both ends in one firing. Cut the U, and trim the pegs to size.

A single wire can be bent to make it self-supporting for soldering. Cut off the excess later.

3. A design may include many pieces of metal that form an open lattice work. With no supporting frame, it is difficult to solder the pieces together one by one.

The best method is to embed the pieces in plasticine. Then mix some superfine plaster of Paris (available from most chemists) with water until it is thick and creamy. Pour it over the piece. When the plaster is dry, remove the plasticine from the back. Clean the metal with lighter fuel. The plaster will hold the metal firmly in place for soldering. After soldering, drop the piece in cold water and the plaster will fall off. Plaster poured down the sink will block it, so take care when disposing of the waste.

4. Charcoal or granite grains are useful for supporting unusual shapes while soldering. The grains should be about 2 mm to 3 mm across. Small white granite grains sold for fish tanks, or carbon grains for fish-tank filters are generally satisfactory.

5. Small metal balls placed on the back of a piece will bridge a gap between pieces that are not quite touching in the design. Make the balls by melting small scraps of metal on a charcoal block. A half ring soldered to the back of a piece will give support to a weak structure.

6. Steel pins will peg sections of a piece to a charcoal block to prevent movement.

Cotter pins or split pins will also hold work. Bend the pins as shown to give an even grip.

Solder inhibitors
To prevent solder flowing to the wrong place, mix rouge powder or yellow ochre with water to form a paste. Paint this carefully where the solder is not wanted. After soldering, remove the paste with a stiff brush.

Sweat soldering
This method can be used when two sheets of metal are to be joined over a large area.

Prepare the surfaces by scoring. This helps to key the surfaces together. Then distribute pallions of solder evenly over one sheet. Heat this sheet only until the solder starts to flow. If the coating of solder is uneven, file off the high spots. Next place the soldered side against the fluxed side of the other sheet. Secure the two sheets together. To join them, heat until a bright line of solder is seen around the edges.

▼ Distribute pallions of solder on one sheet of metal and flow the solder. Fix the two sheets together and reflow the solder.

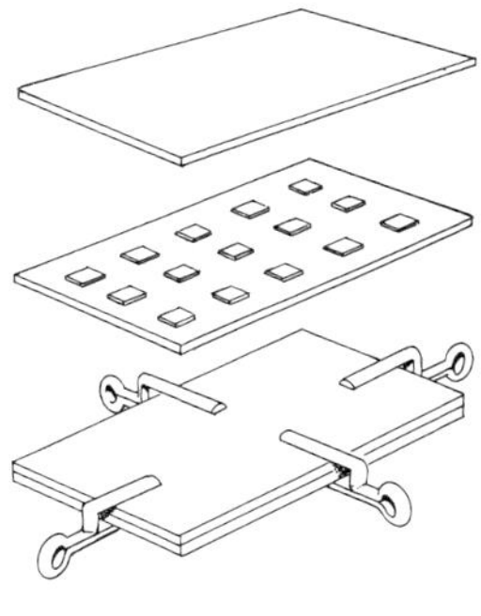

Stick-feeding solder
When a large amount of solder is needed it can be fed from the stick.

Prepare the surfaces, and flux one end of the solder stick. Heat the whole piece with a soft flame until it is hot enough to melt solder touched on it.

Briefly touch the solder stick onto the start of the join. Solder should immediately melt along the join. If this does not happen, the metal is not hot enough.

As solder travels to the hottest point, direct a slightly hotter flame at the metal just ahead of the flowing solder. This will pull it along the seam. At the point where it stops flowing, retouch the solder stick and proceed as before.

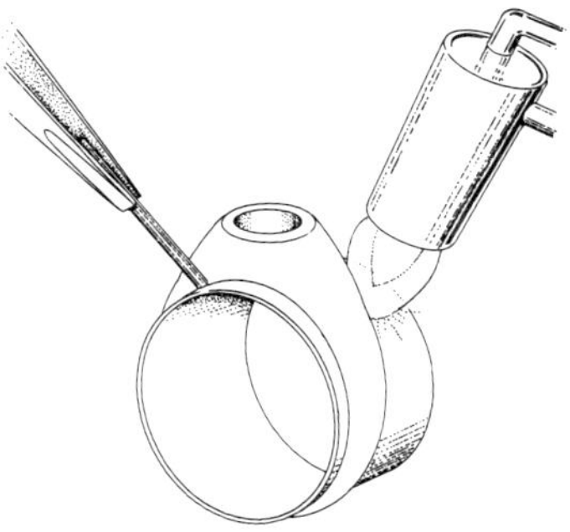

▲ Hold the stick of solder in tweezers to touch it on the seam.

Unsoldering
To unsolder a job, begin by fixing it to the charcoal block. Flux the join to help the solder flow easily and then heat. As soon as the solder flows, remove the unwanted metal with steel tweezers.

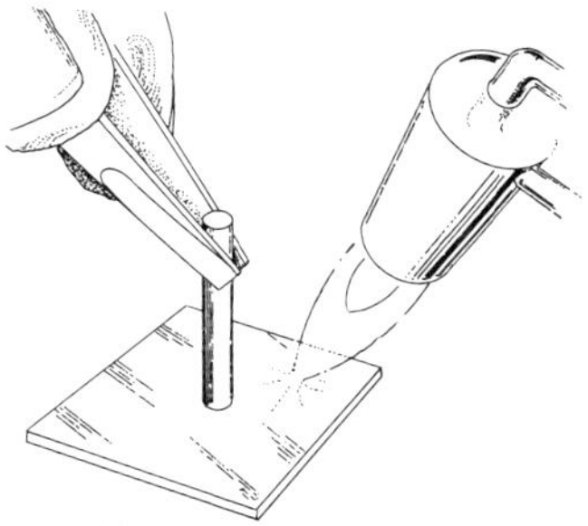

▲ Lift off unwanted parts when the solder flows.

Fire stain
Sterling silver is 92.5% silver and 7.5% copper. When heated in air, the copper on the surface of the silver oxidizes, leaving a dark grey mark called fire stain. This is clearly visible in the first stages of polishing.

Fire stain is only a small fraction of a millimetre thick, so it can be filed off. Alternatively, it can be prevented from forming by excluding air from the metal during heating. To do this, coat the surface with a paste of borax and water, or a paste of borasic acid and methylated spirits. On heating, a dark, glassy, protective surface forms. This is later removed by pickling.

Acid contamination
If work with a porous surface has been pickled in acid, some of the acid may remain in the surface of the metal. This will inhibit the flow of solder. To neutralize the acid, dissolve a few crystals of washing soda in water and boil the piece in this.

The art of decoration

Decoration can change the impact of a piece of jewellery. Texturing an article based on natural motifs can exaggerate organic quality. An important part of a design can be highlighted by enamelling. Darkening low sections of a design will create an impression of greater depth. Engraving can add interest to a plain area. There are many different ways to decorate jewellery so, when designing, consider surface treatments in addition to line, shape, and size. Constantly observe your daily surroundings to find ideas for new decorations, and experiment with different techniques for producing original surface patterns.

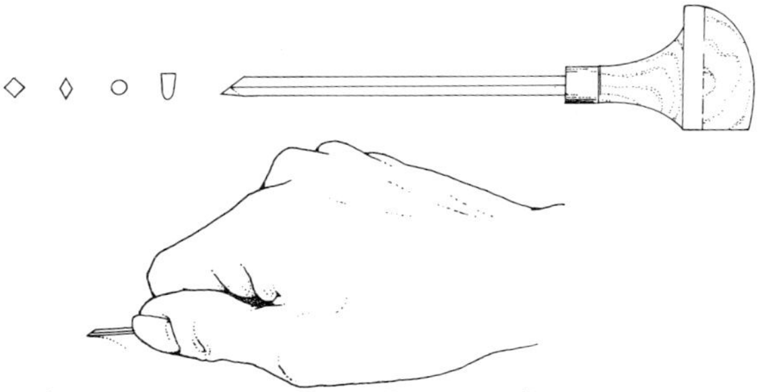

◀ A graver; cross-sections of different-shaped gravers; holding a graver.

Engraving

Engraving is the process of cutting lines with variously-shaped steel tools called gravers.

Tools

The graver is used with the cutting edge almost parallel to the metal. To allow space for the hand, the mushroom-shaped handle has one side removed, and the shaft of the graver is modified (see diagram).

▶ Three alternative ways to prepare the graver.
1. Curve the shaft.
2. Tilt the handle.
3(a). Sharpen two back facets so that the cutting edge is set-off from the shaft;
(b) front face of graver;
(c) side of graver with set-off.

Preparation

Transfer the design to the material (see page 31). Support large pieces on a sandbag, hold rings in a clamp and fix small articles to a block of wood with shellac or setter's cement. Shellac and setter's cement are later removed with methylated spirits.

To engrave

With the handle nestled firmly in the palm of the hand, dig in the point of the graver to the depth required for the line. Lower the handle as far as possible. Push gently, cut about 2–3 mm, then flick out the burr. Engrave the next 2–3 mm in the same way.

Engrave curves in an anti-clockwise direction, at the same time turning the metal towards the graver.

If the graver slips, remove the mark by rubbing it with a burnisher or polished steel rod.

Maintain the cutting point by sharpening only the front face of the graver with oil on a rub stone.

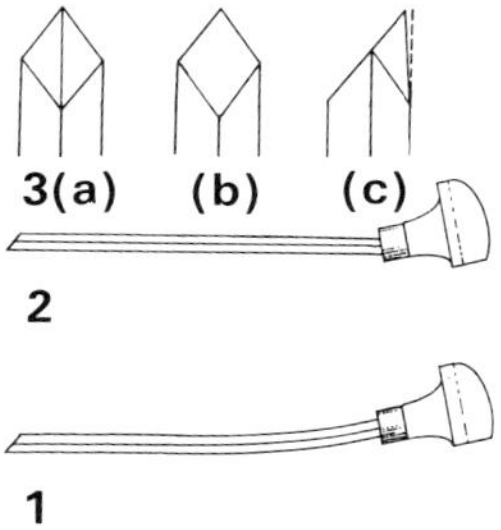

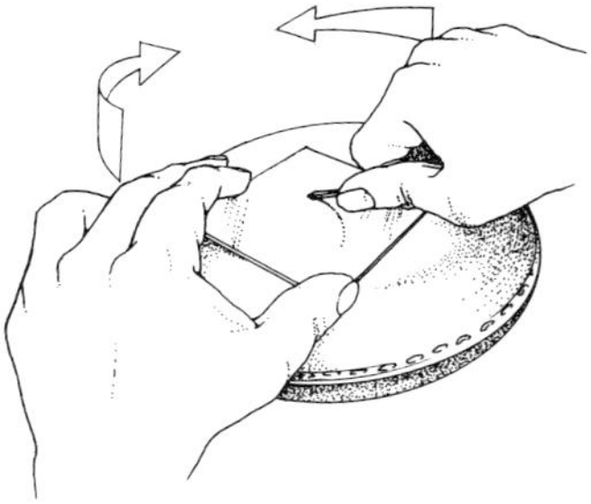

Carving

Metal, ivory, wood and plastics can be carved with engraving tools. Material should be removed gradually, as too much pressure reduces control and may result in a bad slip. Delicate carving leaves a smooth surface. This can be left, or the work can be finished by sandpapering or stoning with Water of Ayr stone, then burnished or polished.

Texturing

Texture on the surface of a piece of jewellery is similar to shading on a drawing. Texture can change the importance of one surface in its relationship to another. It can give metal a natural or organic quality and it can create an uneven surface to contrast with a highly-polished area.

The variety of textures is vast, so devise original textures to suit new designs.

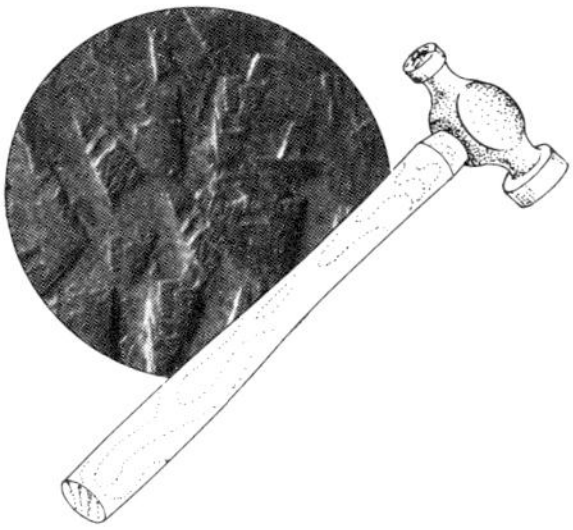

▲ File or saw a pattern into the head of an old hammer. Concentrate the pattern in the centre of the head.

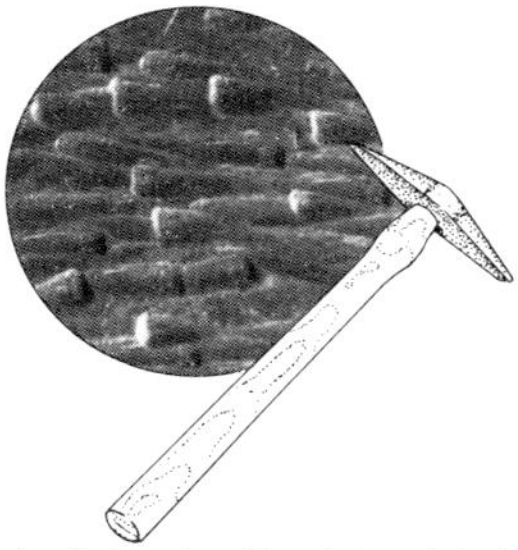

▲ A bark effect is obtained with the wedge end of a hammer. The texture depends on the sharpness of the wedge.

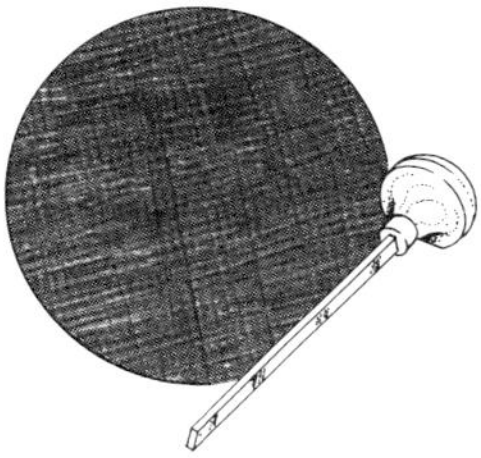

▲ Any shaped graver, used with imagination, will give interesting textures. A line tool, a graver that cuts close parallel lines, produces this texture.

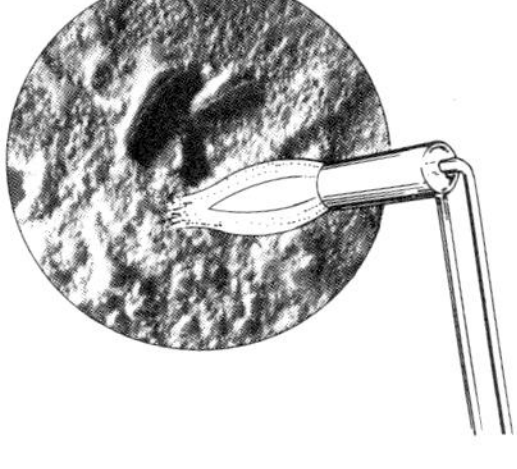

▲ With a blow torch, heat the metal until the surface just begins to melt. Greater heat in one spot will melt the metal and leave a hole.

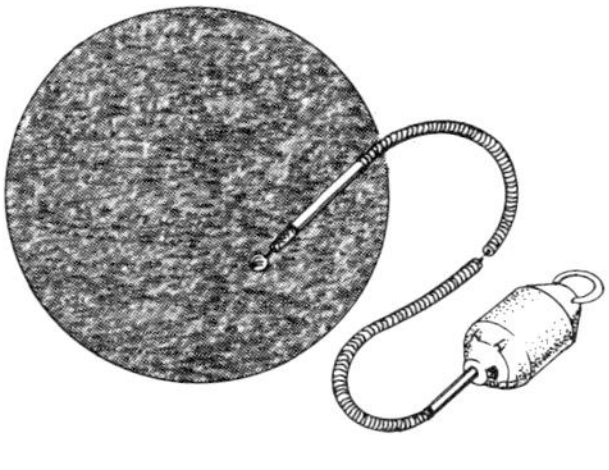

▲ Use a fraize or old dental burr in a pendant drill for a bright texture.

Repeated motifs

Attractive decoration can be developed by repeating one shape throughout a design.

The pearl ring opposite is made up of many small leaves. The amethyst ring is constructed with different lengths of wire. The ovals of the pendant descend to give the impression of a spiral staircase. The round enamel pendant, the enamel tree-brooch and the geometric amethyst brooch also use repeated motifs to achieve an impact.

Identical shapes can easily be cut from tube, called chenier by jewellers. This is made from strip metal. The width of the strip is equal to the circumference of the chenier required plus an allowance for the thickness of metal. So make the width of the strip 3.3 times the required diameter for round chenier. For square chenier, use a strip 4.5 times the length of one side of the square. Also, when making square chenier, a square steel former is used inside the chenier to maintain the shape.

How to make chenier

1. Make the strip into a U-shape (see page 39). Cut a point at one end for drawing.

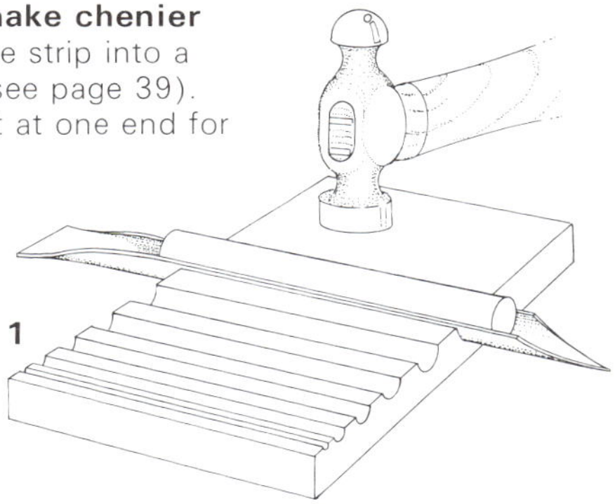

2. Gently tap the sides together to form a rough tube.

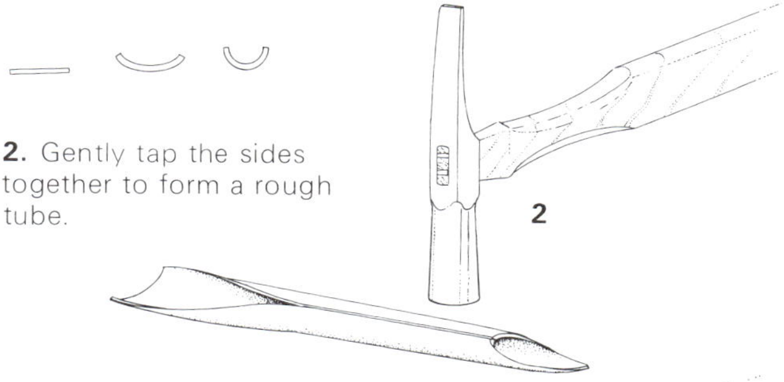

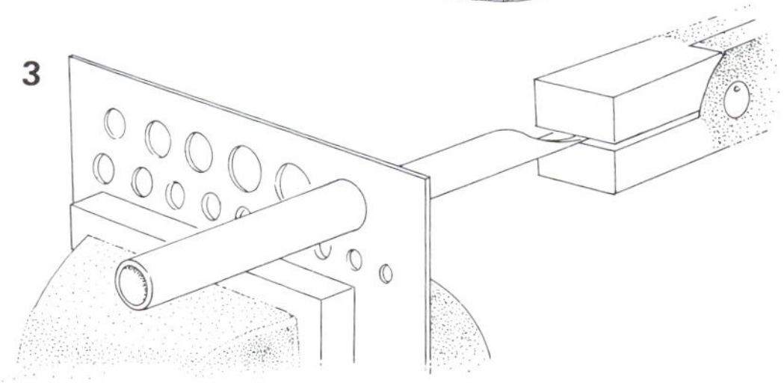

3. Draw this through a round draw plate (see page 62). For square chenier, first make round chenier and solder the seam. Draw this down onto a lubricated steel former through a square drawplate (see page 71). Place the seam on a corner.

◀ Cuff links made with round chenier decoration.

Niello

Niello, a mixture of sulphur and non-ferrous metals, is fused into depressions carved in metal. The blue-black niello contrasts well with silver or gold.

Preparation of metal

Carve the pattern into metal of about 1.8 to 2.0 mm thick. The depression should be approximately 0.5 mm deep.

Clean the metal thoroughly by annealing to get rid of grease and pickling to remove oxide.

Preparation of niello

Choose a recipe from p. 87. Melt the silver in a crucible, add the copper and, when the mixture is molten, add the lead. Stir the mixture with a charcoal or porcelain rod. Remove any impurities from the top with an iron spoon.

Melt the powdered sulphur in another crucible. Work only in a well-ventilated area as sulphur fumes are pungent.

Pour the contents of the first crucible into the melted sulphur, add additional sulphur, remelt and stir. Empty the niello mixture onto a slightly oiled steel slab. This solidifies on cooling. Break up the thin sheet with a hammer and grind the fragments to a powder.

To use niello

Flux the metal with a weak borax solution. Overload the depressions with niello powder. Niello loses about half its volume in fusing. It is better to fire only once, so use adequate powder.

Place the niello-loaded metal on a flat steel sheet and heat from beneath. Do not play the flames across the niello as it will burn, leaving a pitted surface. Do not overfire.

Allow the work to cool in the air. File off the excess niello, then sandpaper and stone the surface until it is smooth.

Niello is soft and should be polished by hand with a flat felt buff and rouge.

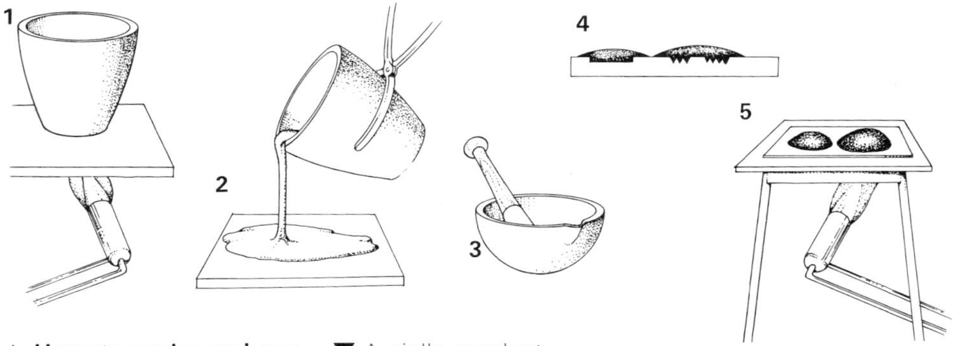

▲ How to make and use niello
1. Heat the crucible from beneath to melt the ingredients.
2. Pour out the niello.
3. Grind broken pieces with a mortar and pestle.
4. Load the metal with niello. If a design includes fine lines, completely cover the surface.
5. Heat the loaded piece from beneath.

▼ A niello pendant.

Chasing and repoussé

Chasing and repoussé are methods for decorating the surface of sheet metal with a relief design. In repoussé, the pattern is punched into the metal from the reverse side. Chasing is worked from the front.

Tools

The same tools suit both processes. The many different-shaped punches used are generally made specifically for each job. The punches are about 12 cm long and 6 mm square in the middle. They taper at each end so that the work can be easily seen. To hit the punch, use a chasing hammer (see page 37). Choose a light hammer as it is better to tap more often than to punch too deeply.

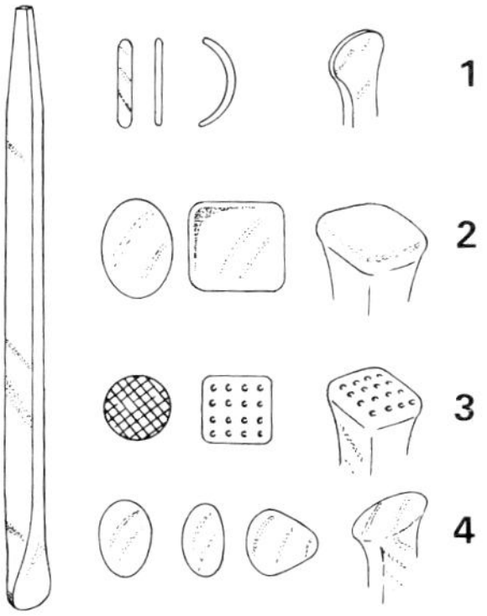

▲ **1.** A line tracer has a narrow face for outlining.
2. A blocking tool is used for gaining depth. It can be any shape but the edges must be rounded.
3. A matting tool has a pattern that can be impressed into the metal.
4. A planishing tool has a larger flatter face for smoothing out relief areas.

To make a punch

Forge or file one end of a piece of tool steel 10 cm x 5 mm x 5 mm into the required shape for the punch. Slightly taper the end to be hit by the hammer. Sandpaper and polish the tool until it is smooth and shiny.

Harden the shaped head by heating it to a bright red colour and immediately plunging it in cold water. The tip should now be tempered to a light straw colour so that it will be hard, but will not be brittle.

▼ To temper, polish the head and play the flame about 2 cm below the tip. The steel will change colour. When the light straw colour reaches the tip, quench the tool in water. Then repolish.

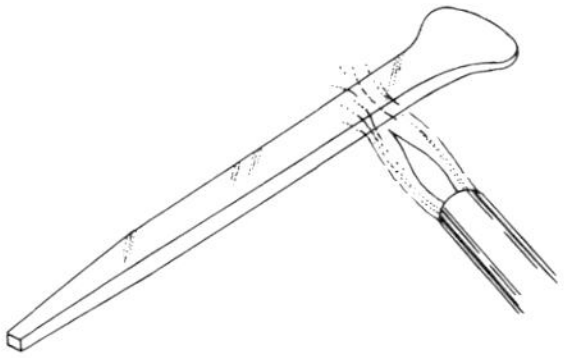

Working surface

Chasers work on a heavy cast iron bowl, almost filled with scrap iron or cement, and topped off with pitch. This is called a bullet. It sits in a leather ring that holds it secure at any angle.

A layer of pitch on a block of wood can be used instead of a bullet.

For a malleable pitch, mix about 2 parts of pitch with 1 part of plaster of Paris powder and add a little tallow.

To work

Scribe the design onto the metal. Soften the pitch with a gentle flame. Warm the metal and fix it in the pitch. Always wet the fingers before touching hot pitch as it may stick to the skin. Allow the pitch to cool before starting work.

Holding the tool as shown, move the heel of the tool across the metal, tapping continually with the chasing hammer. Gradually increase the length and depth of the depression until the desired pattern is obtained.

Remove the work by warming the pitch and lifting the metal with tweezers. Burn the pitch off the metal.

If very high relief is required, the metal may need to be removed from the pitch and annealed several times during working.

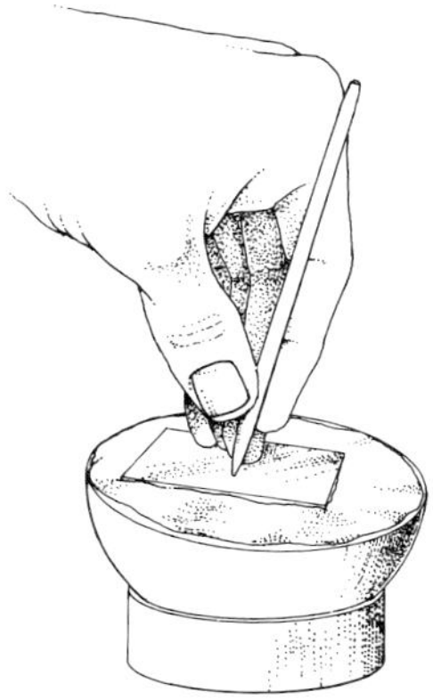

▲ Hold the punch with three fingers and the thumb, using the little finger as a rest and guide.

Enamelling

Enamel is a form of glass that fuses to metal under heat. It can be opaque or transparent and is available in a wide variety of colours.

Metals for enamelling

Gold, copper and silver can all be enamelled. Some enamellers prefer to use only fine silver, especially for transparent colours, as sterling silver can discolour enamel.

Preparing the metal

Jewellery to be enamelled should be soldered only with enamelling solder. This melts at a very high temperature and should not reflow when the enamel is being fired. If necessary, enamel decoration can be made separately and set like stones (see page 57) or pegged on (see page 70).

Enamel will adhere only to a clean, grease-free surface. Anneal the metal to burn off the grease, pickle to remove the oxide and scrub with a clean brass brush under running water to get rid of all traces of acid.

Preparing the enamel

Enamel is purchased as powder or glassy lumps. To reduce the lumps to a usable form, smash them with a hammer between two sheets of paper, then grind the pieces under a little water with a mortar and pestle.

Powder, whether purchased or ground, should be washed. Swill water gently over the enamel and pour it away leaving the enamel in the bowl. At first it will appear milky. Continue washing until the water is clear.

Loading the enamel

For large areas sift dry powder through a fine mesh (a tea strainer is suitable) onto a surface coated with gum tragacanth.

For small areas, position wet enamel with a quill or brush. Tap the side of the metal to settle the enamel evenly. Then draw off the water by touching a piece of tissue or blotting paper to the edge of the enamel.

Apply only thin layers of enamel. Thick enamel will crack off.

Enamel and metal do not contract at the same rate. This causes buckling on cooling. To minimize this, use heavy metal (over 1.5 mm thick). Alternatively, enamel the back. This is called counter-enamelling.

Firing the enamel

Place the dried, enamel-loaded metal on a gauze. (Wet enamel may spit off when heated.) Put the work in the kiln with a kiln fork.

Watch the enamel carefully. It will darken, then melt to a ripply surface resembling orange peel. Remove the work and allow it to cool on a metal surface.

Now apply a second, thin coat of enamel. Fire again, continually checking the enamel. After the orange-peel stage, the enamel will glaze and level out. Remove the piece immediately and let it cool.

Finishing

Enamel from the kiln is described as fire-glazed. This can be left as the finished surface. Alternatively, it can be rubbed with a carborundum stone to give a matt finish, or the surface can be polished with pummice powder after stoning.

◀ Firing a piece of enamel.

The six styles of enamelling

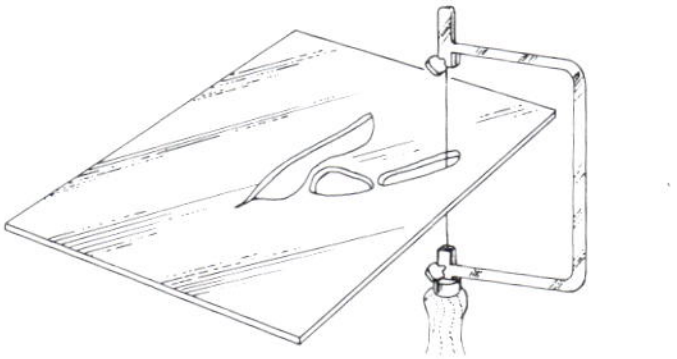

Plique-à-jour
Transparent enamel fills small holes pierced through the metal. The result is like a stained-glass window. Enamel adheres best in rounded holes.

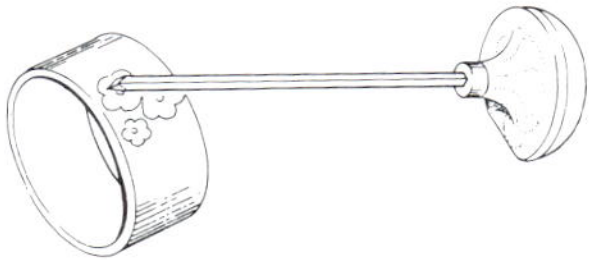

Champlevé
The design is carved to a depth of about 0.5 mm. The depressions are filled with finely-ground enamel and the piece is then fired.

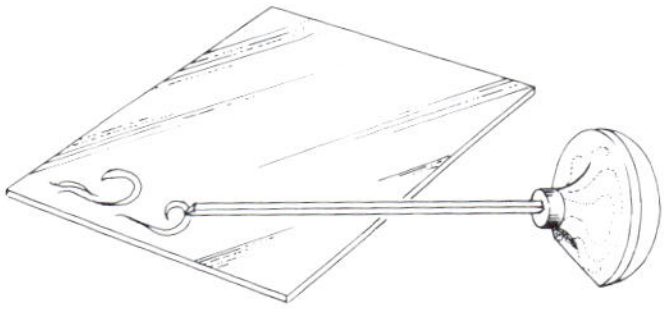

Basse-taille
Transparent enamels are fired over a carved surface. The deeper the carving, the darker the enamel. Varying the depth of carving results in delicate modelling.

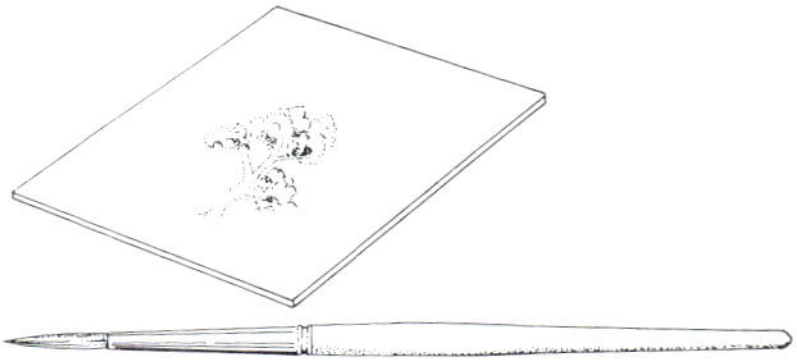

Grisaille
White enamel is painted onto a black background in stages. At each firing, some white sinks into this background. A subtle monotone picture is built up.

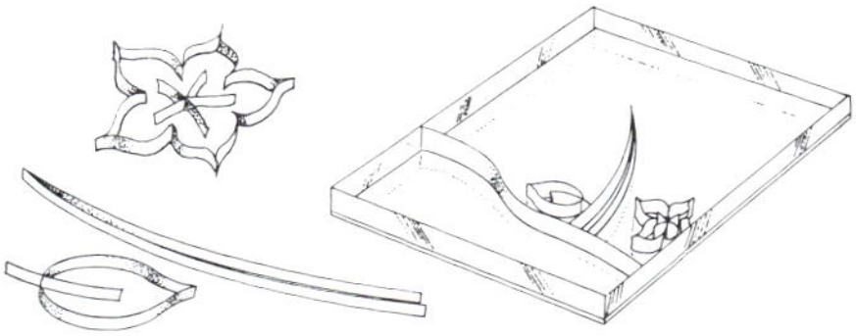

Cloisonné
Cloisonnés (little enclosures) of thin wires are embedded in the enamel with flux. The enclosures are filled with different coloured enamels.

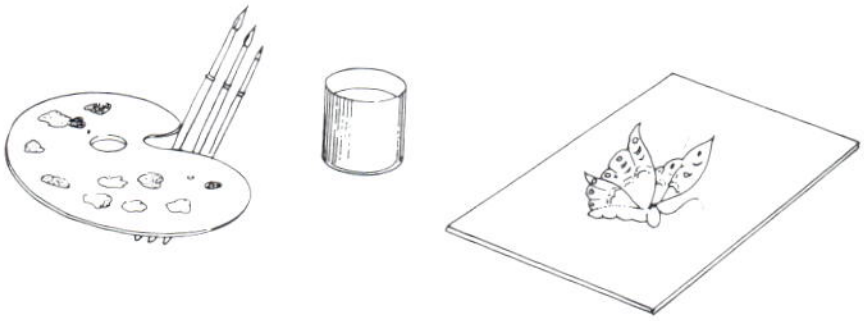

Painted enamel or limoges
Special painting enamel is applied to a white enamelled background using ordinary painting techniques. Many firings are needed to complete a picture.

Colouring metals

The surface of gold and silver can be darkened with chemicals. The use of such colouring agents should be carefully planned as the colour rubs off where it is exposed to wear. It can be used to make depressions appear deeper, to exaggerate texture, or to give a subtle shading.

Method

Clean the metal thoroughly by heating and pickling. Remove the fine silver or gold layer left after pickling with a brass brush. Apply the appropriate darkening agent, then wash the piece and polish the highlights.

Only low carat golds containing copper can be successfully coloured.

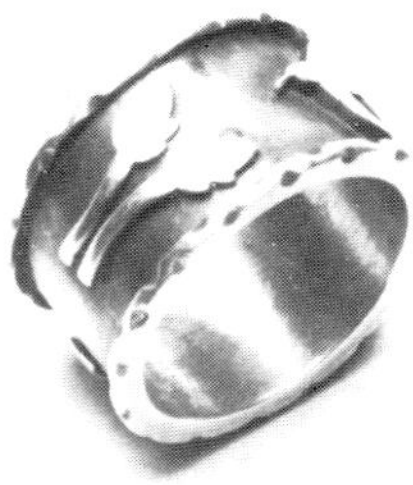

Colouring agents

Work in a well-ventilated area.

For silver

1. To blacken silver, dissolve 2 gm of potassium sulphide (liver of sulphur) in about 50 cc of almost boiling water. Quickly dip the metal in the solution. Redip if necessary. If the solution is too hot, or the work is left in too long, the colour will flake off.
2. To colour silver from yellow to dark brown, place lumps of potassium sulphate in the bottom of a tin. Suspend the job inside the tin, make a small hole in the lid, then replace it and warm the tin gently from the outside. The fumes given off will gradually colour the work, so remove it when the desired colour is reached.

For gold .375 (9 ct) .585 (14 ct)

Use the above chemicals on hot gold.

◀ Different uses of colouring.

▲ An etched neck plaque.

Etching

Etching is the controlled use of acid to eat away metal. A surface may be etched for decoration, or in preparation for niello or enamel (pages 50, 52).

To etch

Warm the metal to melt an acid-resisting substance, such as dark ball ground, onto the surface. Beeswax and shellac are suitable resists if the design has no fine lines. See p. 87 for details of acids.

Scratch the pattern through the resist. Only exposed metal will be attacked. Immerse the metal in the appropriate acid for the pattern to be etched to the required depth. It may take several hours.

When etching is complete, remove the resist. Acetone will remove beeswax and ball ground, methylated spirits will remove shellac.

Inlaying

Inlaying is the technique of embedding one material flush into the surface of another.

Tools

The tools required are a flat graver, a small wedge-shaped punch and a hammer. Make the punch from steel about 6 cm long and 5 mm square. File a small wedge at one end.

Inlaying wire into sheet metal

To inlay wire, first cut a track with a flat graver so that the wire will fit tightly and protrude slightly.

Open out the base of the groove with the wedge-shaped punch by moving it along the corners of the groove and tapping gently.

Anneal the wire thoroughly, then lay it in the slot and tap it into place.

If the wire becomes hard and springy during hammering, anneal it. It should then lay easily in place.

File the whole surface flat.

Inlaying sheet metal

Either carve out the area to be inlaid, or pierce a hole in one sheet of metal and sweat-solder it onto another sheet. Push back the bottom edges of the depression with the wedge-shaped punch.

The sheet to be inlaid should be slightly deeper than the hole. Anneal it thoroughly and position it in the hole.

Place a flat steel block over the whole surface. Hammer the block to press the metal into the depression.

Inlaying other materials

Wood, bone, ivory, shell and plastics can be inlaid into metal or each other in a similar way. Because such materials expand and contract at different rates, they generally have to be secured with glue. Also, the holes and inlay pieces have to be fitted very accurately.

Make the inlay a tight fit, and encourage the material into the depression with a flat-faced punch or hammer. A block of steel over the inlay will help to give an overall even pressure.

Inlaying tortoiseshell

Thin silver is easily inlaid into tortoiseshell. Boil the tortoiseshell in salty water for about an hour to make it soft and pliable. Warm two steel plates. Quickly lay the warmed silver on the soft tortoiseshell and sandwich it between the two steel plates. Squeeze the plates enclosing the tortoiseshell between the jaws of a vice and leave it until it is cool.

The silver is pressed into the surface of the tortoiseshell and held in place by the contraction of the tortoiseshell as it cools.

1

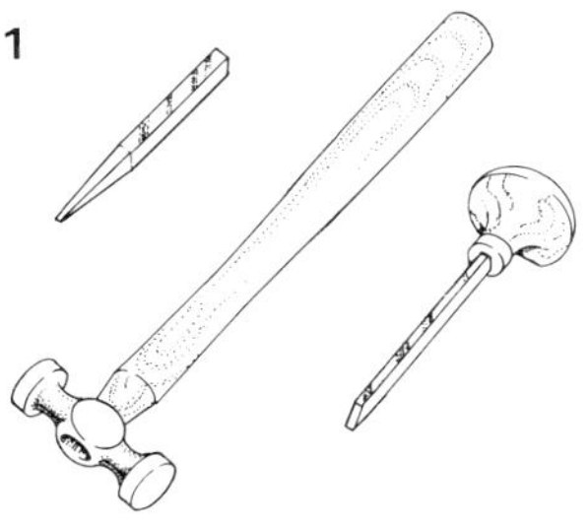

2

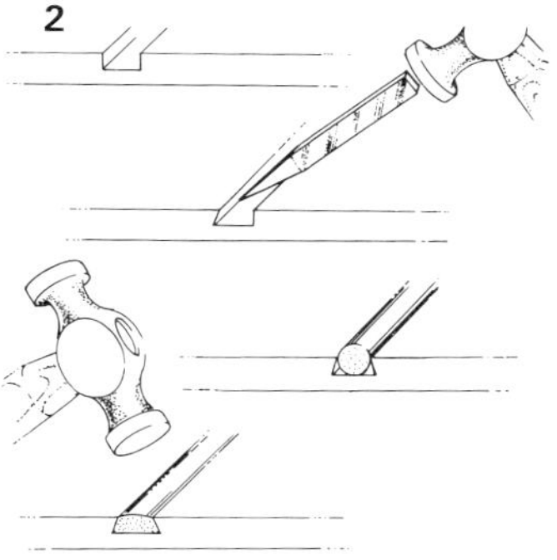

3

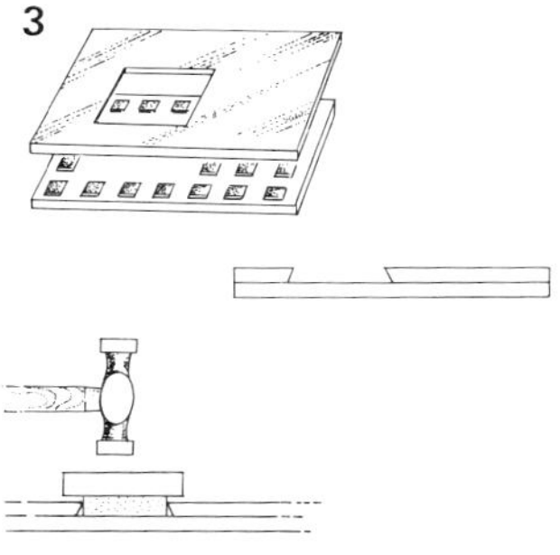

4

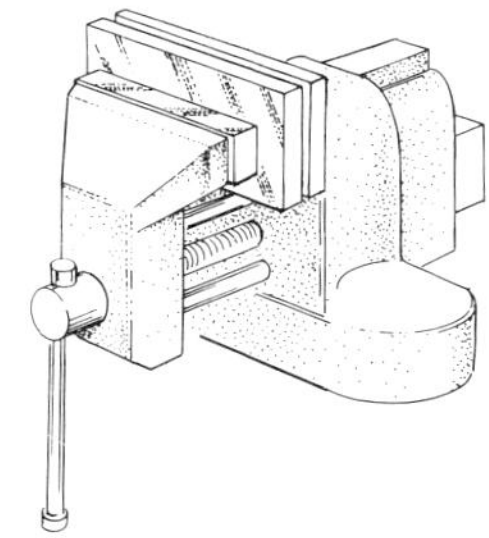

◀ **1.** Tools.
2. Stages of inlaying wire.
3. Stages of inlaying sheet.
4. Squeezing steel plates and tortoiseshell in a vice.

Mounting and setting stones

A mount is the metal that holds a stone. Setting is the process of pushing the metal over the stone to keep it permanently in place. A mount, called a collet when made for one stone, can be simple or elaborate. It supports the stone from beneath, prevents sideways movement of the stone and has sufficient metal above the stone for setting. The thickness of the mount depends on the design, the stone and the metal. Silver, being softer than gold, needs to be thicker than gold in a mount for the same sized stone. Appearance is also important. A heavy metal surround may detract from the stone. So the metal thickness is a compromise between strength and appearance.

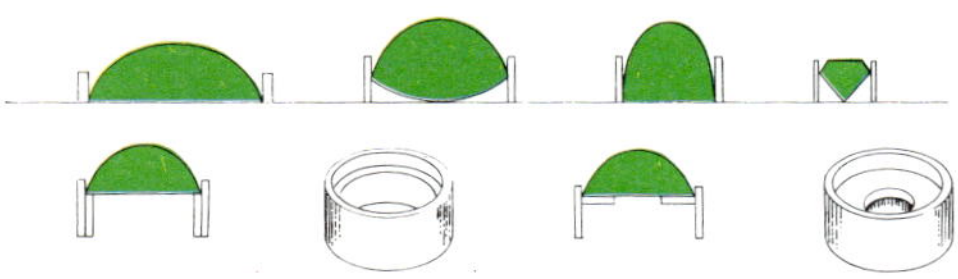

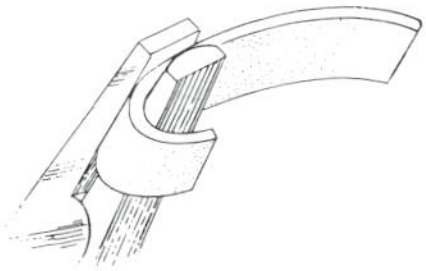

Simple rub-over collets

These are suitable for most stones. The height of the collet depends on the slope of the sides of the stone. The surrounding metal has to be high enough to push over the edge of the stone to hold it.

Sometimes, a stone needs to be set above the level of the rest of the work, so insert a bearer to support the stone at the required height. A vertical bearer is sufficient for most jobs but, if the stone is thin or weak, a horizontal bearer will give greater support over the base.

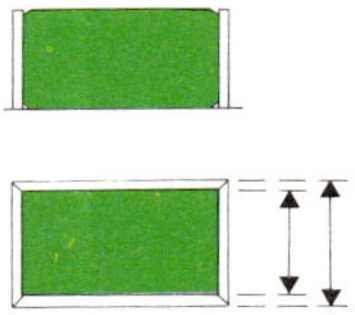

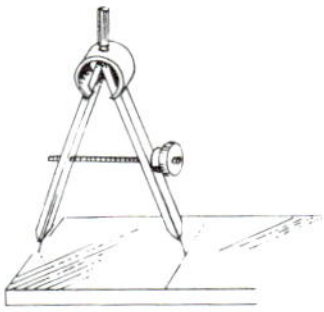

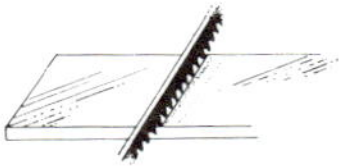

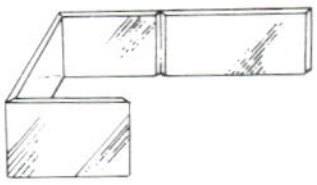

Making a collet

Cut a strip of metal long enough to go around the stone. Bend the strip to the shape of the stone with pliers. The stone should just drop into the collet. Solder the join. If the collet is too small stretch it with a metal hammer on a triblet. If it is too large, remove a section of metal.

Square or rectangular mounts

Square stones usually have a slightly bevelled edge, over which the metal is pushed to secure the stone. To determine the length of metal strip required, measure the length of each side and to each measurement add twice the thickness of the metal. This is to allow metal for the corners (see diagram).

Making a square collet

Open dividers to the length of the collet. Transfer the measurement to the strip and mark it with a saw. In the same way, mark the width of the collet, then the length and width again.

File along the saw marks with a square needle file until the strip is filed almost through. File each end to an angle of 45°. Bend up the metal to form the collet and solder each corner.

▶ Holes for pavé set stones

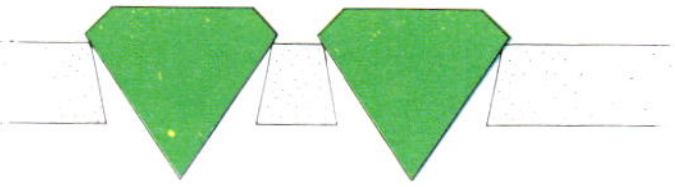

The girdles (edges) of the stones should be almost touching. Drill a hole, pass the piercing saw blade through and open the hole for the stone as shown. Use the side of the blade in a stroking fashion. Once this technique has been mastered, a perfect hole can be opened and positioned using only a saw.

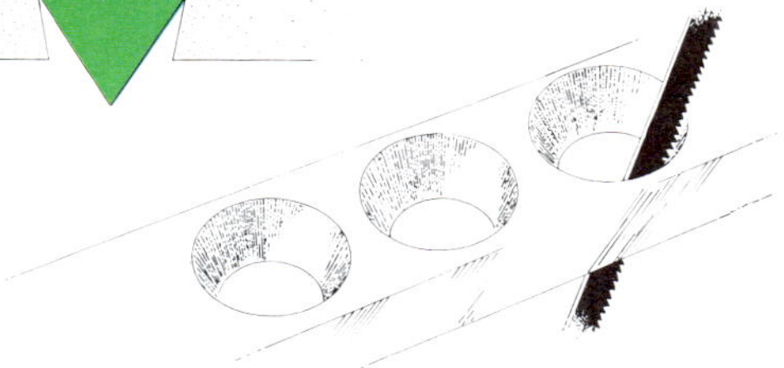

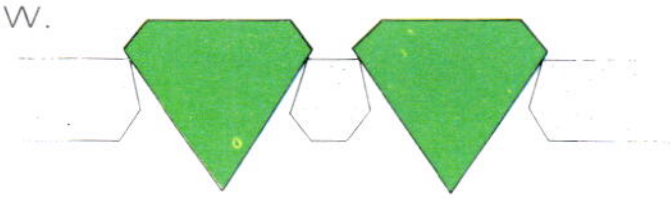

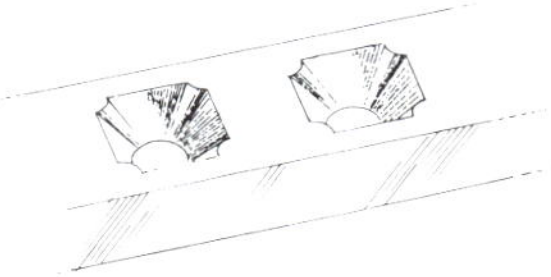

◀ Back holes

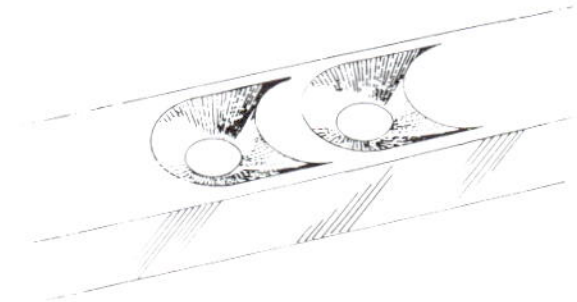

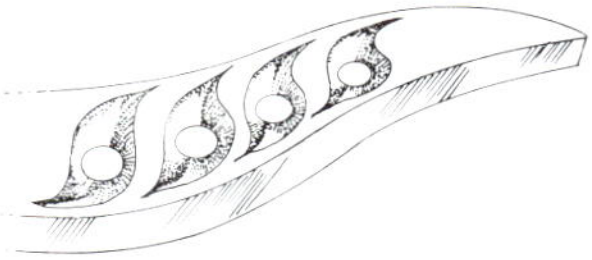

The backs of the holes are opened up to allow more light to reach the stones and to lighten the setting. The back holes can be any shape but should not weaken the setting. To get the sharp corners, slope the blade into the corner and, using the edge of the blade, gradually ease off the metal. Work towards the corner from each side.

▶ Baguette mounts

Begin with a rod of metal, the same width as the stone and slightly deeper. Mark off the length of the stone plus 1 mm ($\frac{1}{2}$ mm at each end for the claws). Saw out the top third. Drill a hole, pass a saw blade through and open out the top hole. Turn the rod over and open the back hole. Saw off the mount.

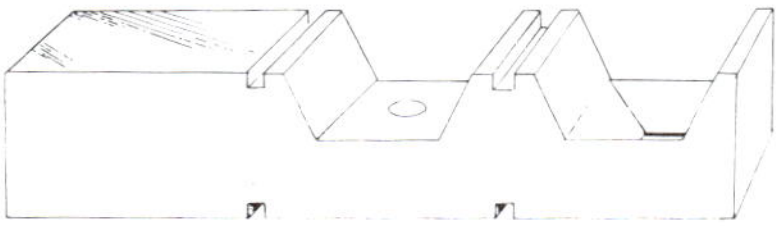

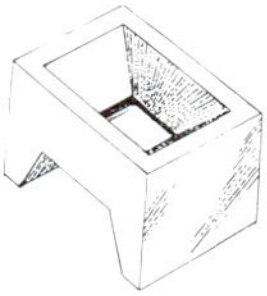

◀ Crown collets

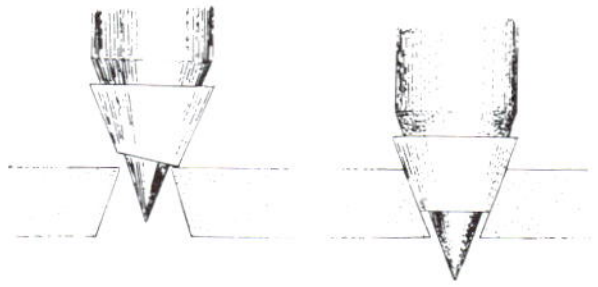

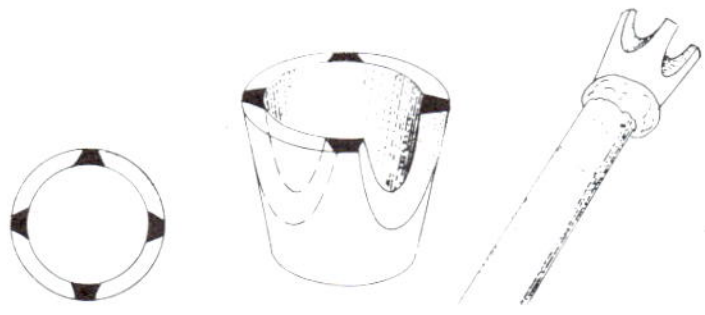

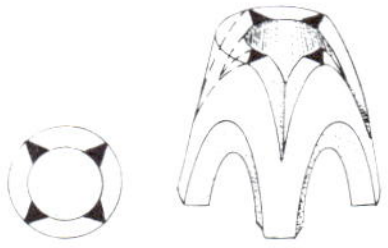

Bend a strip of metal to a flat curve. With round-nose pliers, bend up a collet. Solder the seam, and correct any unevenness with a collet plate and punch. For easier handling, attach the collet to the end of a pencil with shellac. Saw out the claws and nick up from the base with a three-square needle file.

◀ Wire collets

Wind wire around a suitably-sized rod. Make support wires as shown. For the claws, make a U-shape or cross. Solder the claws between the top and bottom rings (or marquise shapes). Bend up the claws and trim them to length (allow enough for setting); saw out the centre cross of the round collet.

▶ Simple claw collets

Make a pattern similar to the shape shown so that, when the claws are bent up, they will be high enough to hold the stone above the collet. Put the shape on a lead cake and tap a punch on the centre. This will cause the claws to be pushed up. Generally, metal about 1 mm thick will be suitable.

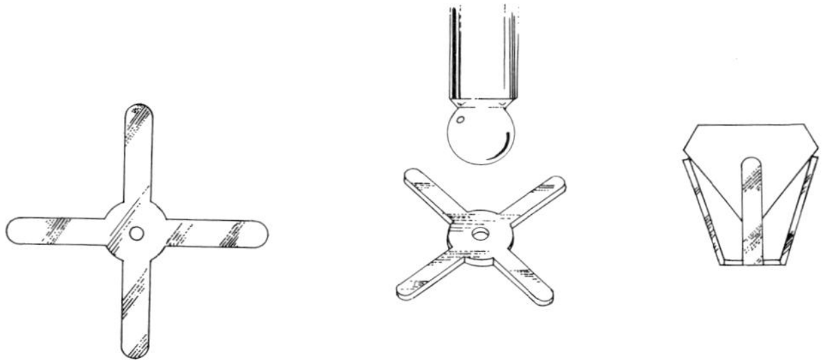

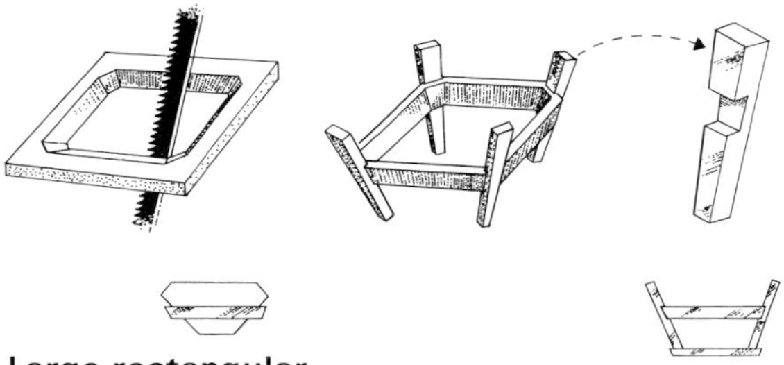

◀ Rectangular or emerald collet

From metal about 1.5 mm thick, saw a shape with slanting sides to fit the stone. File the outside to the same slope. Note the position of the stone in the collet. Make the base a little smaller using the same technique. Cut and fit the claws as shown. When soldering, secure them with binding wire or hold them with tweezers.

▶ Large rectangular setting

The support can be made as shown. Mark out one side of the stone. Draw two lines to represent the slope of the collet. Draw in the circle and mark the position of each corner and side around the circumference. Cut out this pattern and file a groove at each corner to bend up the collet. Or transfer it to a strip of metal as shown.

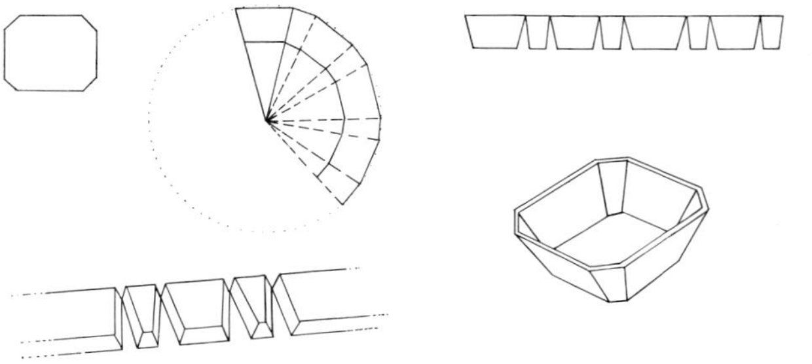

Setting stones

The mount has been prepared so that the stone just rests on the top edge of the metal. To set the stone, make the fine adjustments necessary to bring the stone into position for setting. Then either push metal over the edge of the stone, or raise little grains of metal to secure the stone. Check that the stone is level, at the correct depth and evenly spaced between other stones.

Tools

The main tools are (1) a spit stick for cleaning metal from around stones; (2) a half-round scorper for raising grains; (3) a ball stick for cutting bearers for stones to sit on; (4) a flat scorper for trimming claws; and (5) a pusher for pushing metal over stones. The ends are ground down to leave only a small face for sharpening on an arkansas stone.

To set the stones, the work is held secure on a setter's stick. A 15 cm length of broom handle will do. Melt setter's cement onto one end. To use the stick, make the cement pliable in a soft flame and push the warmed metal into it. With wet fingers, push the cement up to support the work. (Hot cement sticks to dry skin.)

Rub-over settings

If necessary, trim the inside of the collet with a ball stick so that the stone sits firmly on the bearer. Use the pusher to ease the metal against the stone and then over its bottom edge. First, push the metal at the ends and sides of the stone to secure it. Check that the stone is level and central, then gradually ease over the rest of the metal. When the metal is firmly against the stone, trim the top edge with a spit stick taking care to cut only the metal and not mark the stone.

Claw setting

With the ball stick cut notches in the claws to support the girdle of the stone. Click the stone into place. Push the claws upright, then trim the outside of the claws with a flat scorper. Ease the claws down onto the stone with the pusher.

Grain setting

Cut a bearer for the stone to rest on into the side of the mount with the ball stick. The stone should sit firmly about one third of the way down the side of the mount. To raise a grain, dig the half-round scorper into the metal about 1 mm from the edge. Push down and forward and lever a grain of metal up from the surface. Dig the scorper back in the same place, push forward and twist to the left to lever up the left side of the grain. Do the same to the right side. It is the base of the grain pushed forward over the girdle of the stone that holds it in place. The top of the grain can, therefore, be trimmed or decorated. Trim away the excess metal behind the grain with a spit stick.

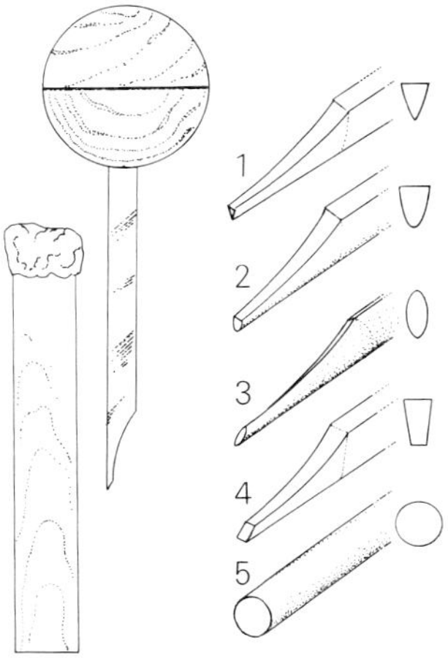

1. Tools.

2. Rub-over setting.

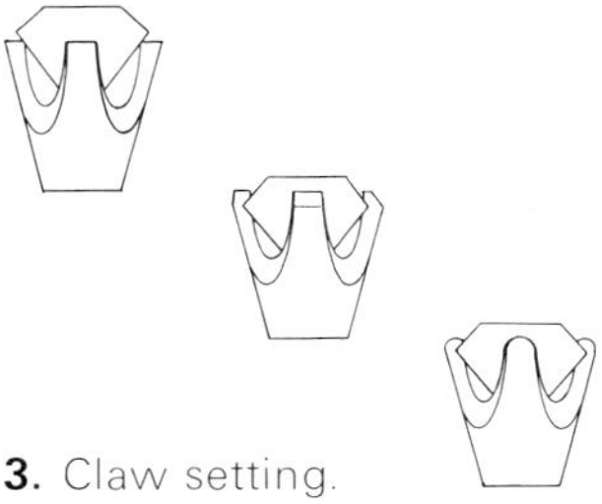
3. Claw setting.

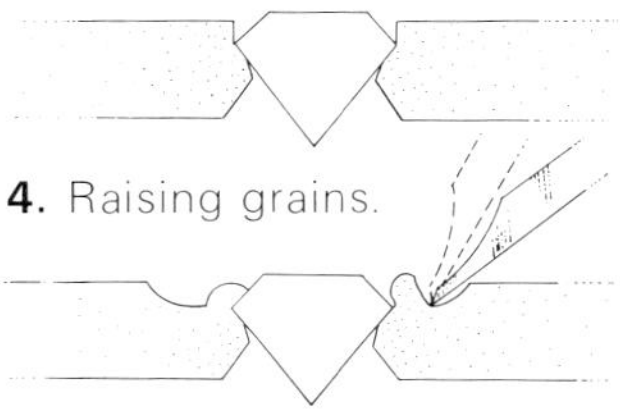
4. Raising grains.

Rings

Rings were first made popular by the Romans, who often wore them on every finger. Today, rings are still commonly worn. Most rings are round, but this is not necessarily the best shape, so consider other possibilities when designing. Also take into account the purpose of the ring. A wedding band which is to be worn every day should be designed to be comfortable, and the decoration should be such that wear will not destroy the appeal of the ring. Alternatively, a ring for special occasions can be delicate or very large. Be adventurous and original in designing and, where applicable, devise new mounts to suit the design.

Tools

The size of a finger is found with a ring size. Allow two sizes larger for a wide band. Check the size of a finished ring on a ring size stick. A ring clamp holds a ring secure for working.

To find the length of metal required, wind binding wire around the ring size stick or the finger. Add $1\frac{1}{2}$ times the thickness of the metal to allow for bending; or bend up a longer strip, overlap the ends and saw through both layers of metal.

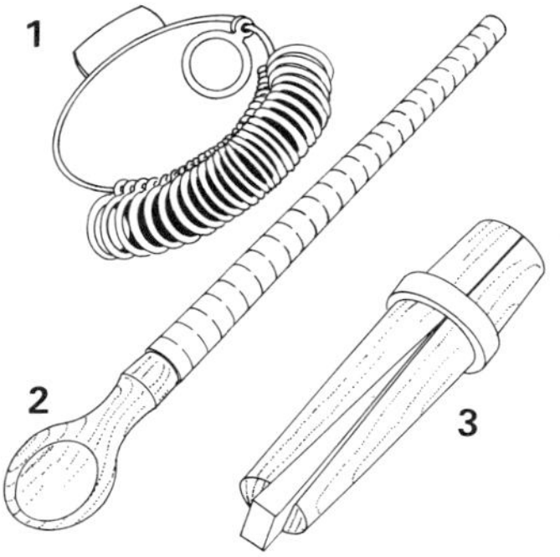

To make a ring round

Tap the ring round on a ring triblet, a tapered rod of steel. To use the triblet, wedge the small end in a hole in the edge of the bench and support the triblet against the chest. This leaves both hands free to work.

Slide the ring as far up the triblet as possible, then move it back a little, so that the metal surface is flat against the triblet. If this is not done, the ring will be hammered to the same taper as the triblet.

Tap the ring with a wooden or hide mallet, while continually rotating it with the other hand. Remove the ring from the triblet, reverse it, replace it, and continue tapping. The ring will soon be round. If the ring is too small (by up up to about $1\frac{1}{2}$ sizes) use exactly the same method and tap the ring with a metal hammer. This will gradually stretch the metal. If the ring is much too small, solder in extra metal. The metal added should stand proud of the surface so that it can be filed back to the right shape.

Enlarging a ring

To enlarge slightly, tap on a triblet if hammering will not harm the decoration. Otherwise, heat the ring gently to show up the previous join. Check that the hall mark does not cross the join, then saw down the dark solder line which appears and insert extra metal as shown. File the new section to shape.

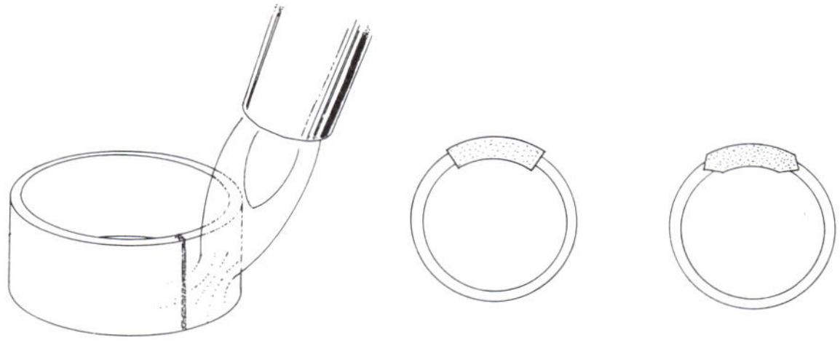

Making a ring smaller

Heat gently to reveal the solder line. Saw down the solder line, then remove enough metal to resize the ring. (About 1.5 mm is equal to one size.) Sometimes, to protect the top decoration, the back of the ring has to be pulled in. The ring is no longer round, but will still fit.

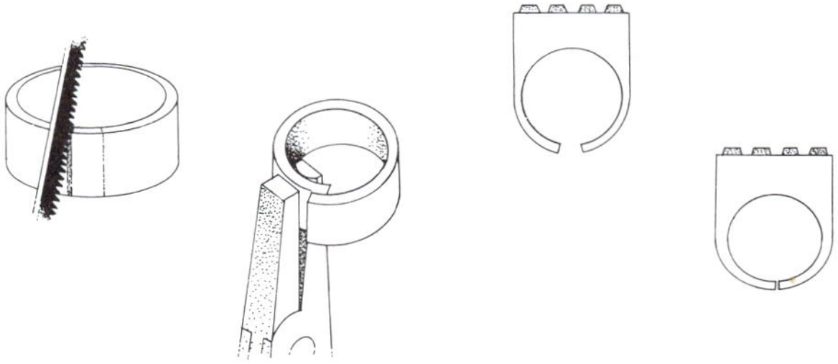

◀ A variety of rings
The ring at the top is made from three differently coloured, swaged bands of gold. The propeller on the ring on the left turns when the hand is moved. The ring at the top right contains two small boxes which open. The silver ring (middle left) is bent up from a flat sheet of metal. The two rings in the centre show different types of collets. The square ring in the bottom left-hand corner has a bead which rolls around the decoration but will not fall out. The ring in the bottom right-hand corner has plique-à-jour enamel. The sapphire ring at the bottom centre is made by fusing metal.

Wire and chain work

Many simple and attractive pieces of jewellery can be made from wire alone. Using a steel drawplate, the diameter of wire can be reduced, or the cross-sectional shape changed. For instance, round wire can be made triangular in cross section by drawing it through the appropriate graded holes of a triangular drawplate. Wire can also be twisted for use as decoration. To do this, one end of the wire is held in a vice. The other end is secured in a hand drill and the handle is then turned. One or a number of strands of any shaped wire can be twisted in this way and as long as the wire has been evenly annealed, the twist will run smoothly down the wire.

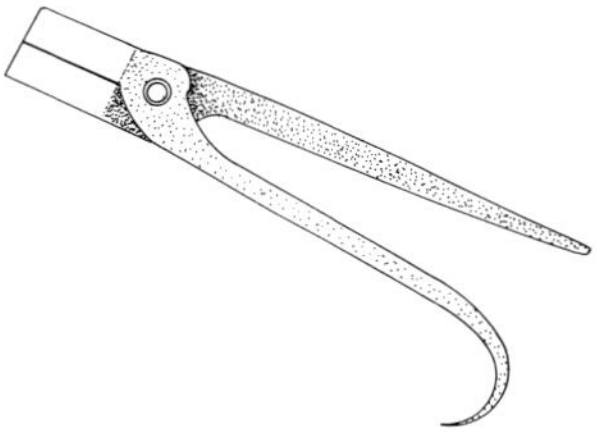

▲ Draw tongs.

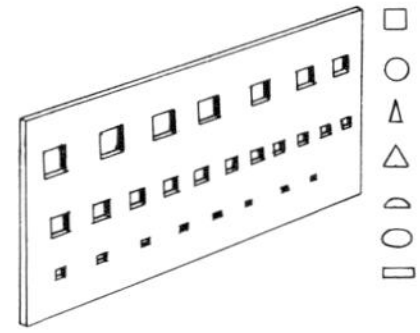

▲ A square draw plate. Several shapes are available.

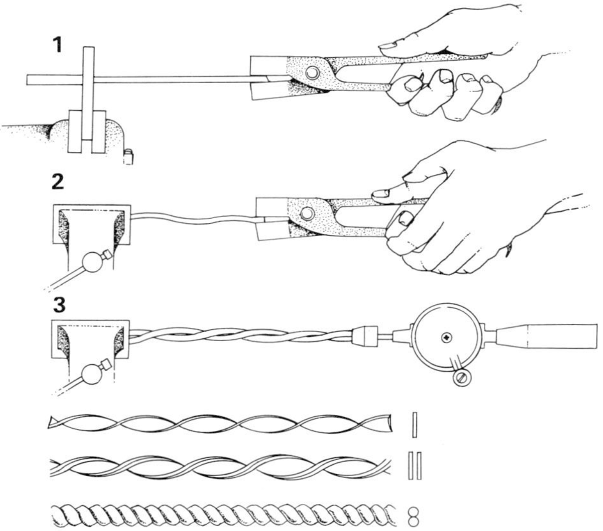

▲ **1.** Drawing wire.
2. Straightening wire.
3. Twisting wire.

Drawing down wire

To reduce the diameter of wire, first anneal it. Either hold the wire in tweezers and blow the flame along the wire, or coil it and heat with a large, soft flame.

Secure the drawplate in a vice. File a 15 mm tapered point on one end of the wire so that it can be passed through a hole slightly smaller than the wire and gripped by the draw tongs. Lubricate the wire by warming it and running it through beeswax or paraffin wax. The wax will melt onto the wire.

Grip the wire in draw tongs with both hands. The hook on the handle stops the hand slipping off. With arms extended, lean back using the weight of the body to pull the wire. This ensures a firm, even pull. Work from larger to smaller holes.

Straightening wire

Anneal the wire, fix one end in a vice and give one sharp, even, pull. The wire will be straightened and work-hardened.

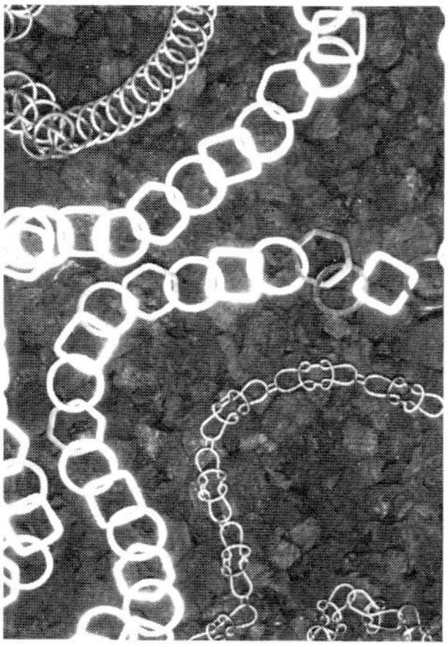

To make a chain

Choose a mandrel of the size and shape required for the links. Anneal the wire and wind it around the mandrel. It is advisable to wrap brown paper around first so that the links slide off easily. Anneal the wire on the mandrel and burn out the paper at the same time. Move the wire down to the end of the mandrel and saw each ring off one by one. Adjust the ends of the links together with two pairs of pliers.

To solder, isolate the join and blow the flame across the link so that previous joins do not overheat or the solder reflow.

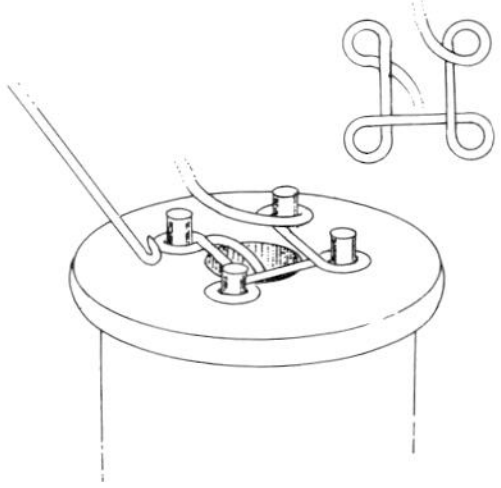

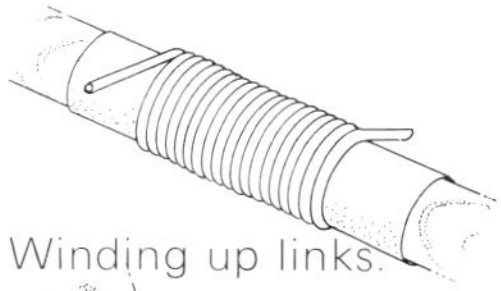

1. Winding up links.

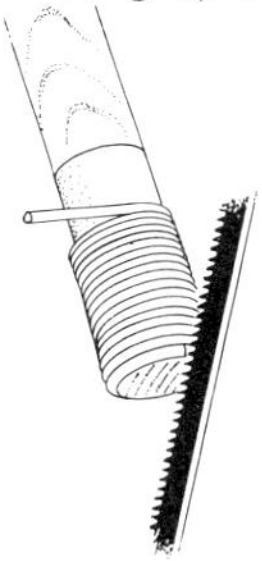

2. Sawing off links.

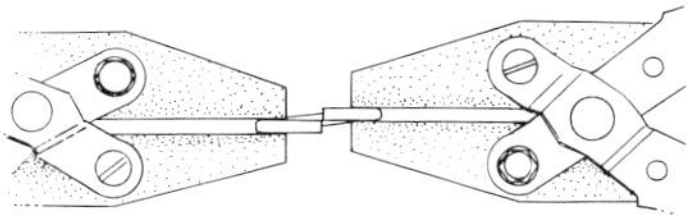

3. Adjusting the ends of a link.

4. Soldering the links.

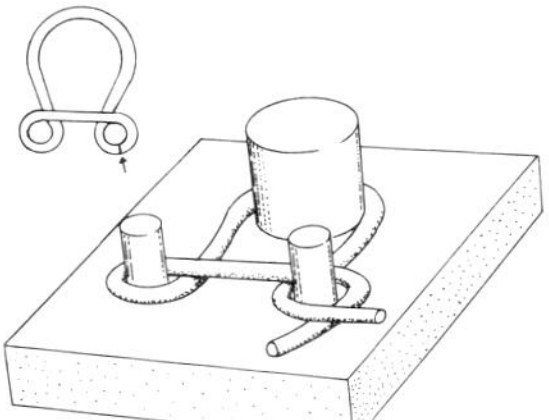

▲ A former

To wind up the links in the chain illustrated, make the former with one large rod and two small ones. Drill holes in a block of wood and fix the rods securely. Anneal the wire and wind it around the rods as shown. Try different formers to get other shapes.

▲ A mandrel

Mandrels can be bought in various shapes, or they can be made from steel or wood. Oval nails make good oval mandrels.

French knitting with wire

For the chain shown above, first hammer four headless nails into a cotton reel. The nails should be evenly spaced and close to the edge of the hole. Draw the wire to the smallest hole in the round drawplate (usually about 0.3 mm will be small enough). Anneal the wire carefully, then wind it around the four nails in the way shown. Next wind a loop around the first nail so that the nail has two loops. With a small crochet hook, or hooked wire, lift the bottom loop over the top loop, and drop it off into the centre hole. Wind a loop around the next nail and repeat. Continue until the chain is the length required.

Unusual materials

Silver and gold are not the only materials from which jewellery can be made. Many natural materials, plastics and resins could be used and even the use of other metals can lead to unusual effects. The oxides formed on titanium and stainless steel under heat are brightly coloured, so it is worthwhile investigating the properties of such metals. In general, the tools used for silver and gold are suitable for other materials as well, but if larger pieces are carved, heavier wood carving tools are needed. Experiment with different materials and design the jewellery to suit the qualities of each material.

▼ Some other materials that could be used for jewellery: **1.** Horn. **2.** Teeth. **3.** Tortoiseshell. **4.** Ivory. **5.** Coral. **6.** Mother of pearl. **7.** Ebony. **8.** Wood. **9.** Beads. **10.** Buttons.

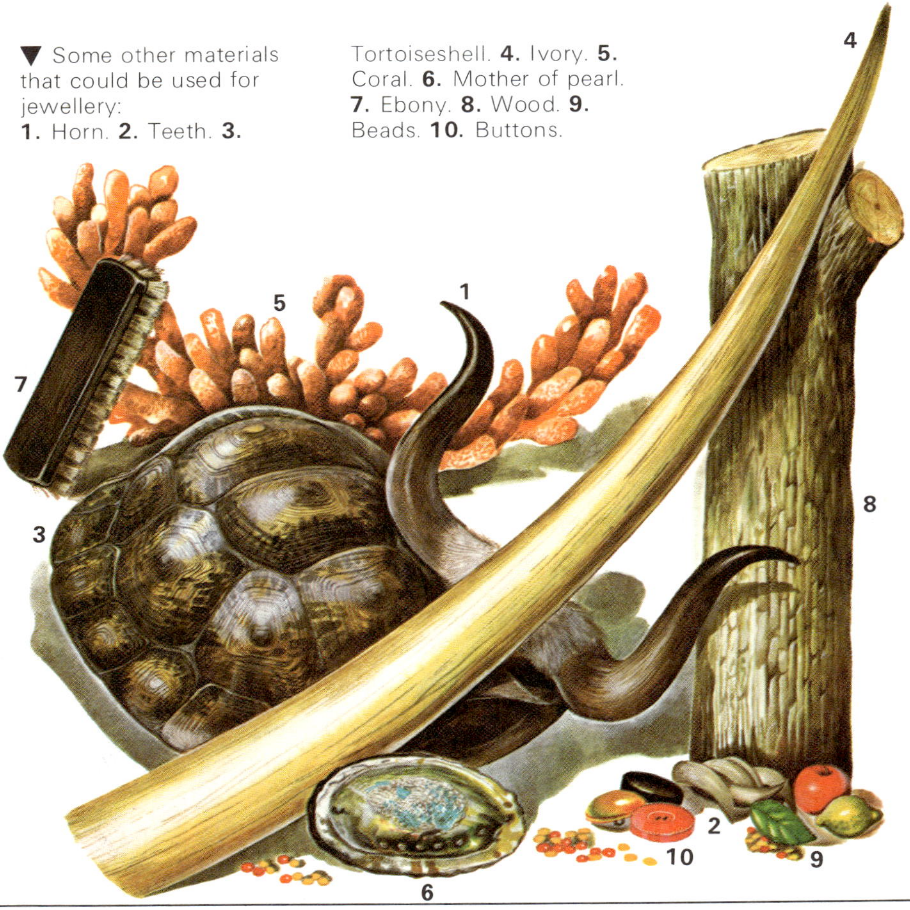

▶ The bracelet at the top right is carved from lignum vitae. The pendant on the top left is made from ebony and ivory and hangs on string. Both of these pieces are finished with fine sandpaper, then polished by hand with a mixture of beeswax and turpentine. The middle pendant is made up of layers of silver and African black wood riveted together (see page 70). The brooch is tortoiseshell inlaid with silver (see page 55). The ivory pendant in the bottom left-hand corner is carved and polished by hand. The little gold decorations are riveted through the ivory. The beads on the orange pendant are threaded on silver thread and suspended from twisted, orange silk thread. Beads can also be stitched onto a leather backing, or tied into macramé (the art of decorative knot tying). The ring is plastic.

Different materials will be available in different areas, so investigate to see what can be found. Junk shops are often a good source for supplies, especially for ebony which was used on brushes, desk sets and boxes. Also, tortoiseshell can be found on the backs of old mirrors.

Fittings and findings

Findings is the name given to all the attachments that pin or fasten jewellery. These include such things as joints, catches, snaps and ear-clips. Many of these can be purchased already made up, but sometimes a piece of jewellery requires a specially-made finding. Findings can be hidden, disguised, or made to be part of the design of the piece. For instance, the snap on a pearl necklace is commonly very ornate so that it can be worn at the front as a focal point; but the snap on a bracelet is often so well disguised amongst the links that only those familiar with the bracelet know where to find it. Joints, pins and catches are usually hidden.

Joints for pins

1. A simple joint is made from chenier. File a groove into a back plate so that the chenier sits firmly in the groove. On the seam side of the chenier, mark off the positions for the three knuckles with a saw. Cut half way through the chenier at the two centre marks, then file the centre section down to these cuts. This centre section is not used, but acts as a bridge to hold the other two pieces in place for soldering. Position the notched-out chenier, seam-side down, in the groove and solder it. Cut out the bridge. Fit another knuckle into the gap. Solder the pin to this knuckle as shown. Rivet up the joint.

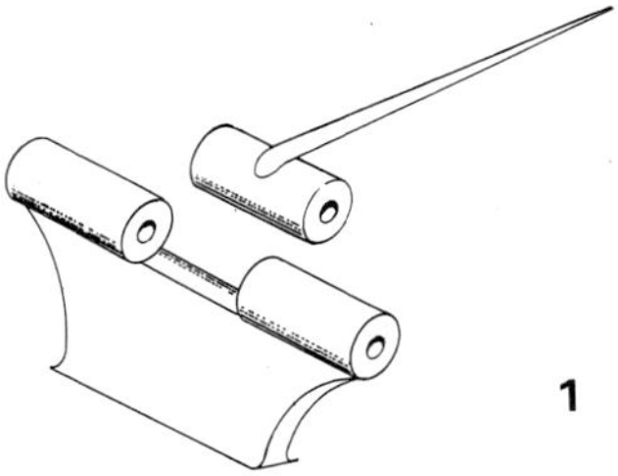

1

▲ Chenier joint.

▼ Filed joint.

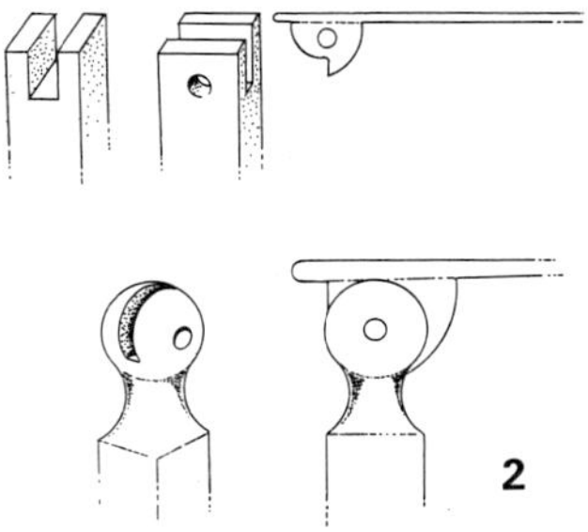

2

2. Where the joint needs to be very small, it can be filed from a solid block.

Cut a slot as shown. Make the small flag piece on the pin to fit into the slot. The tail of the flag piece stops the pin from dropping down. Put the flag piece in position and drill a hole for the rivet, as shown. File up the joint so that it forms a small neat ball standing on a stem. Rivet the pin and flag piece into place.

3. Bend a U-shape around a flag piece. File up the joint and flag piece as shown. The front of the joint stops the pin dropping down.

A pin is always fitted so that, when it is riveted in position, it has to be pushed down to secure it in the catch.

4. One way to keep the pin in the closed position is to fit a cross spring. Solder a piece of chenier to the brooch, thread a straight wire through, then bend it to form a cross. Lay this flat to do up the pin, and stand it up to keep the pin in place.

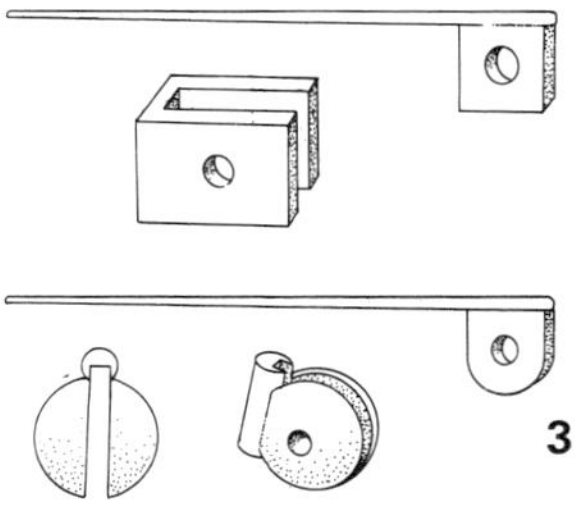

3

▲ U-shaped joint.

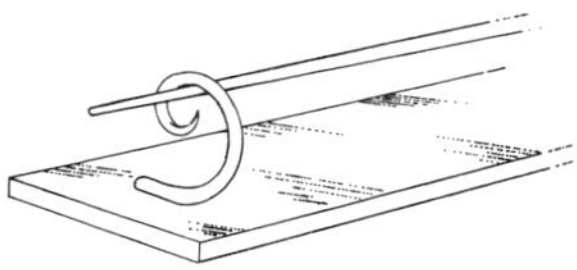

▼ Cross spring.

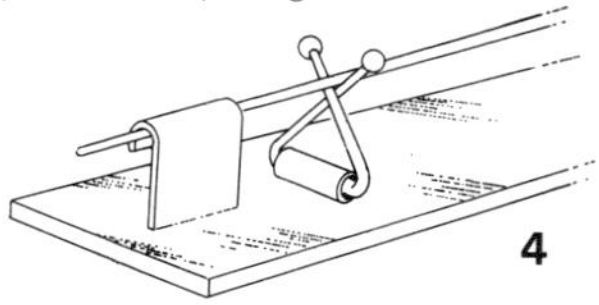

4

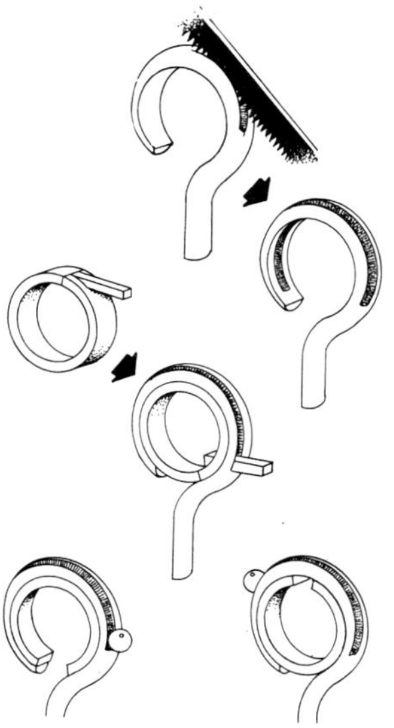

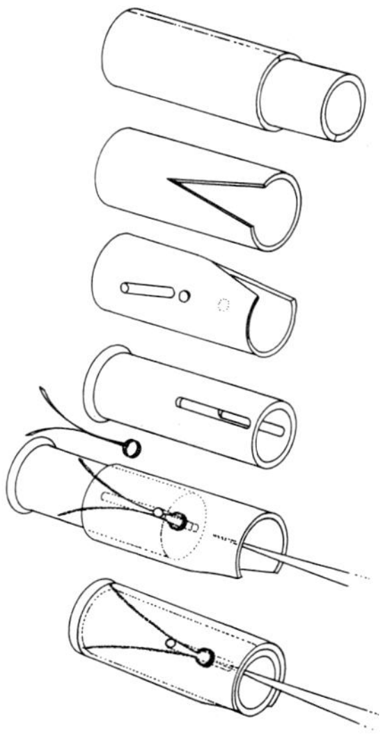

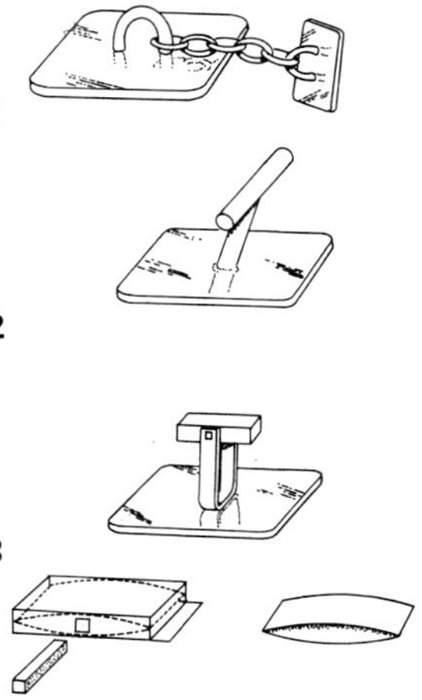

▲ Safety catch
Bend a D-shaped wire into a hook and cut a slot down its back. Make chenier to fit snugly into the hook. Make a thumb piece to fit through the slot in the hook, then cut a slot in the chenier from the seam as shown and solder the thumb piece into the chenier. Open the hook, fit the thumb piece through the slot, then close the hook around the chenier. Put the thumb piece at the back so that the chenier seam is at the opening of the hook. Open out the seam for the pin. File the sides flush, and shape the hook. Carefully solder a small piece of chenier over the thumb piece and shape it.

▲ Tiffany catch
Make two pieces of chenier, one that fits snugly inside the other. File a slot in the larger one and drill a hole to take a peg. Solder a ring to the smaller chenier for a thumb piece, and cut a slot to fit around the peg so that when the peg is in position through both pieces of chenier, the inside one can slide in and out. Make a spring from nickel silver or thin steel wire (a guitar string is suitable), fit it around the peg and open it out just over the top of the thumb piece. When the catch is closed, the spring holds it shut, and the inner chenier encloses the pin.

▲ Cuff link fittings
1. Make a chain to attach the back fitting to the front.
2. If a fixed back is used, fix it at an angle to make the cuff link easier to put on and remove.
3. For a spring fitting, rivet a small box containing the spring between the two arms. When these fittings are purchased, the box is supplied separately. Assemble the fitting after the arms are soldered into place because heat weakens the spring. To make the spring, mill or hammer a strip to work-harden it and bend it as shown. Insert the spring in the box and push the end shut. Do not solder as heat weakens the spring.

1. This is the style of ear-clip normally purchased. Assemble by riveting up the hinge (see page 70) and adjust the spring action by raising or lowering the centre tab of the ear-piece.

2. File three pieces of chenier. Attach the back plate to the centre chenier for fixing to the ear-ring. Solder the centre rod through the centre chenier. Then solder the ear-piece wire to the other two pieces of chenier. This also forms the spring.

3. Make a U-shape from D-wire to fit down the hole in the chenier. When the D-wire is in place, rivet a small peg through the chenier to prevent the wire falling out.

4. For pierced ears, make a butterfly or sea scroll fitting. The scrolls spring against the wire to grip it. Or bend up a small hook.

5. Make a simple box snap as shown. Bend up the blade from work-hardened metal. The double thickness of metal should just slide beneath the notched front plate of the box. Cut the top blade so that, when the snap is pushed into place, the top blade springs up behind the front plate.

6. Make a side snap as shown. The top slot and the side notches locate around the blade and pegs when the snap is shut. The long slots have to be wide enough to allow the blade to be pushed into place.

1

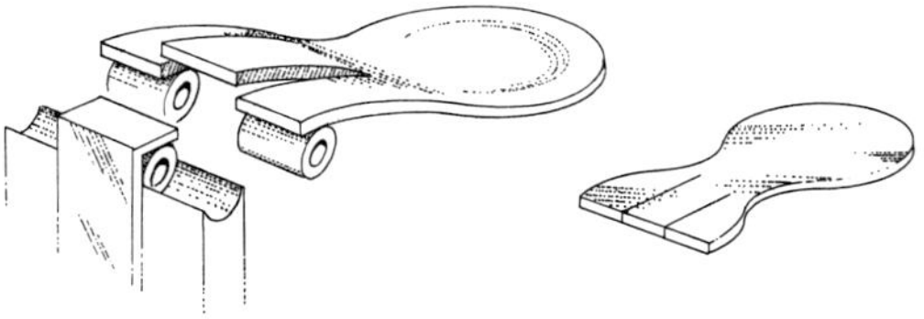

2

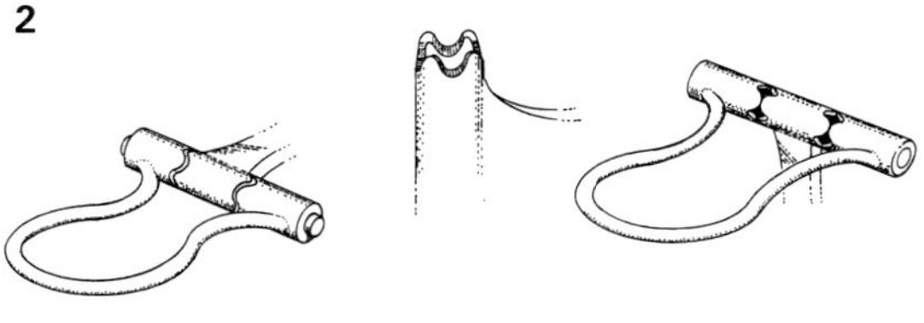

3

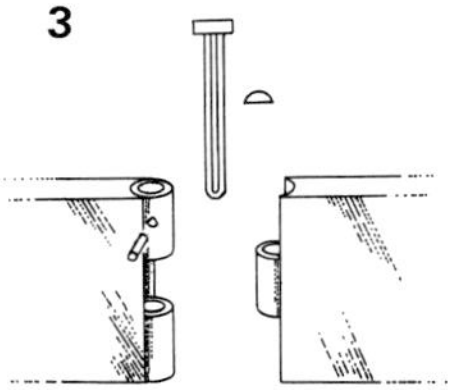

4

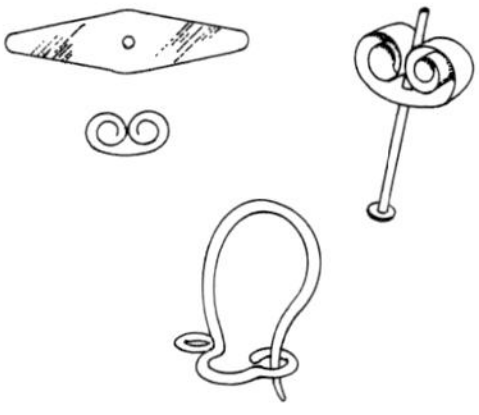

5

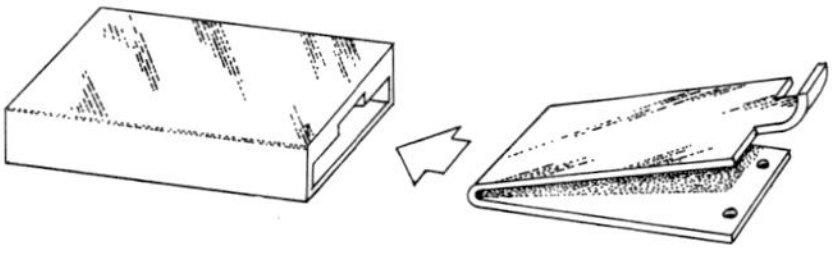

6

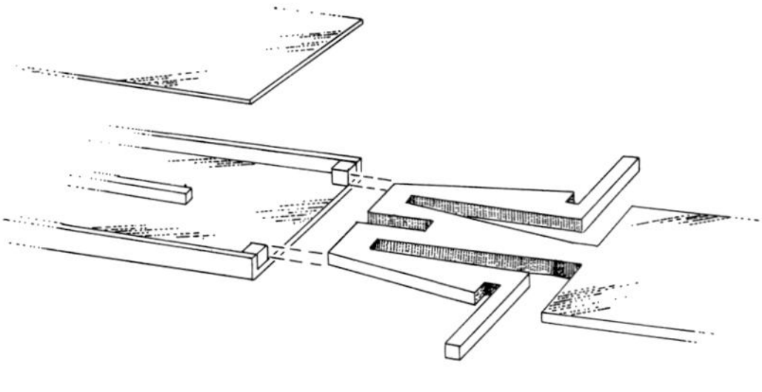

Jointing

The jointing for necklaces and bracelets has to be strong, but completely flexible. Each link needs to move only slightly for the whole bracelet to bend freely. To allow for this slight movement, file a small bevelled edge at the back corners, as shown.

1. Solder rods across the links so that a plate (about 0.5 mm) will fit under the rod. Solder a plate under one rod, thread it under the rod of the next link and bend the plate back over both rods. Tuck it down behind the first rod and carefully solder it in place. Use a solder inhibitor (see page 45) to prevent the previous solder joins from reflushing and fixing the joint.

2. A similar method, but in this case, thread wires through the holes in the next link.

3. Notch out one bar to fit the tab on the opposite bar. Make the joint by riveting the two bars together.

4. Solder small plates onto one end of one link as shown. Fit these into the next link, then drill holes through both the link and the plates. Rivet the plates to the links.

5. These links are called dumb-bells. This is one way to make a bracelet or necklace completely flexible. Make small half-round loops by winding up rings and cutting each ring in half. Solder the loops onto all the places to be jointed. Melt a small ball onto one end of a wire. Thread the wire through the two appropriate loops, then melt a small ball on the other end to stop the wire falling out. Always make sure that all parts of the necklace or bracelet are supported, as one missed link makes the whole structure weak. Sometimes rings can be used instead of dumb-bells.

1

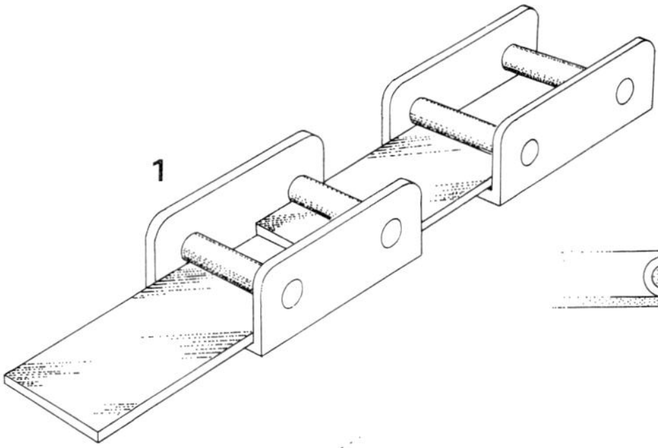

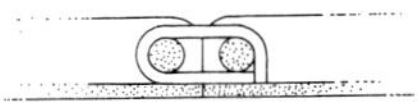

2

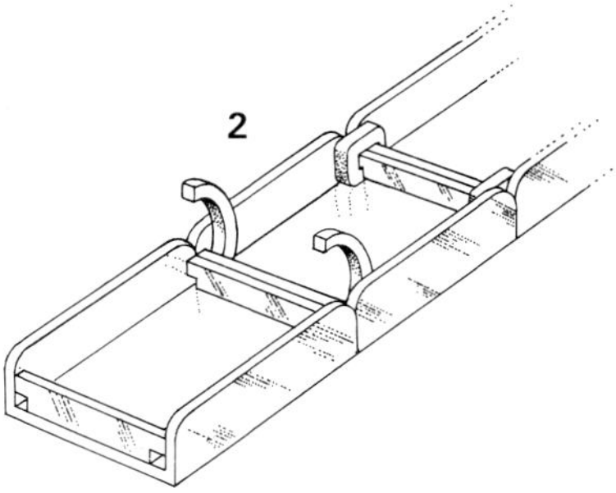

3

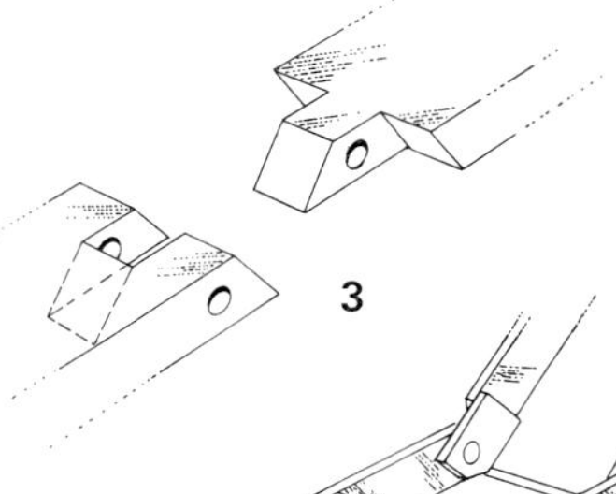

4

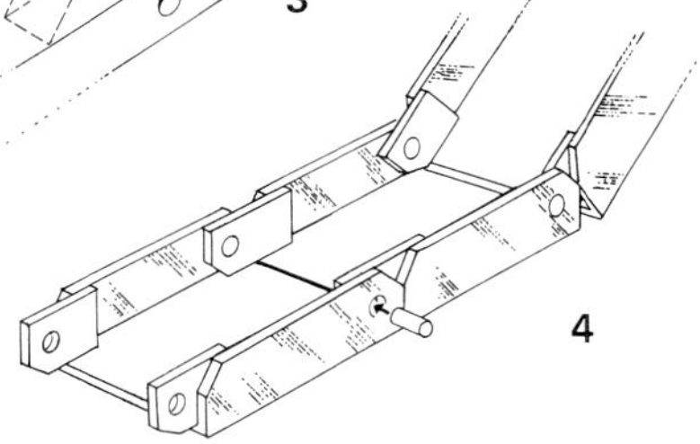

5

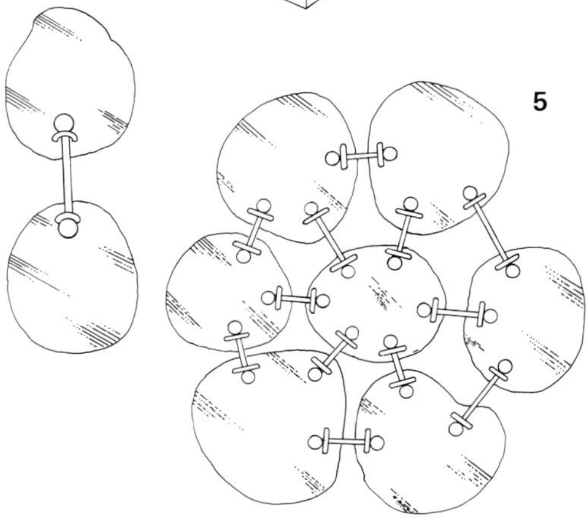

Joining without solder

There are many occasions when solder cannot be used to join the parts of a piece of jewellery! This is because either the pieces will burn, or the solder in previous joins might reflow. Sometimes, for more convenient setting and polishing, a job is made in several sections and assembled when all stages are completed. Rivets and pegs are useful for attaching parts together. Sections are riveted if a hole can be drilled through all parts, a wire passed through the hole and hammered at each end to prevent it falling out; or pieces are pegged if pegs can be soldered to one side of a job and secured through locating holes on the other side.

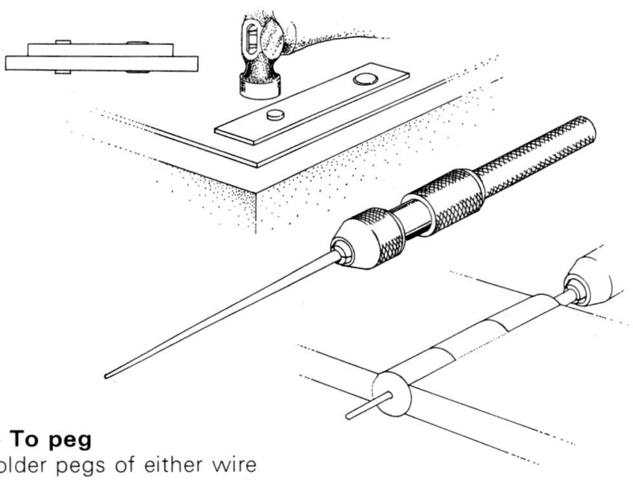

◀ How to rivet
Drill a hole through all sections to be joined. For the rivets, use wire which fits tightly into the holes. Push the wire through and trim it off, leaving $\frac{1}{2}$ mm protruding at each end. Support one end against a steel block and tap the other end to extend the wire over the edges of the hole. Repeat for the other end. For hinges, use a broacher to make a tapered hole. File the rivet wire to a matching taper and screw it into place with a pin vice. The pin will then be tight.

▶ To peg
Solder pegs of either wire or chenier onto one section of the job. To locate the pegs in the opposing section, either drill holes or solder on chenier to fit over the pegs. Then, to secure the top section, hammer out the pegs using the same technique as for rivets, or open out the chenier over the edge of the hole. Countersinking the hole with a fraize helps to make the pegs more secure. It is generally better to use square pegs, as these prevent sideways movement.

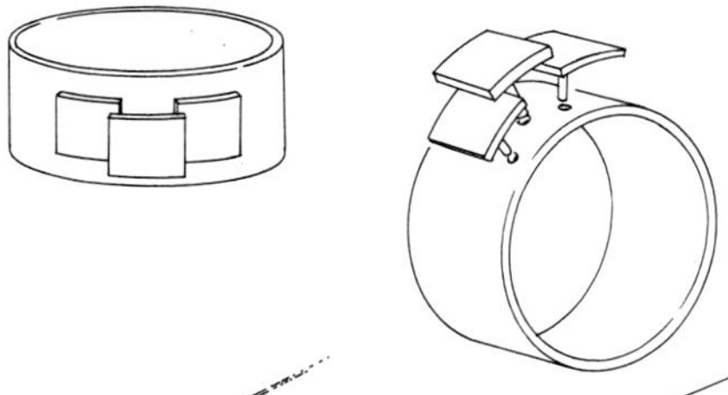

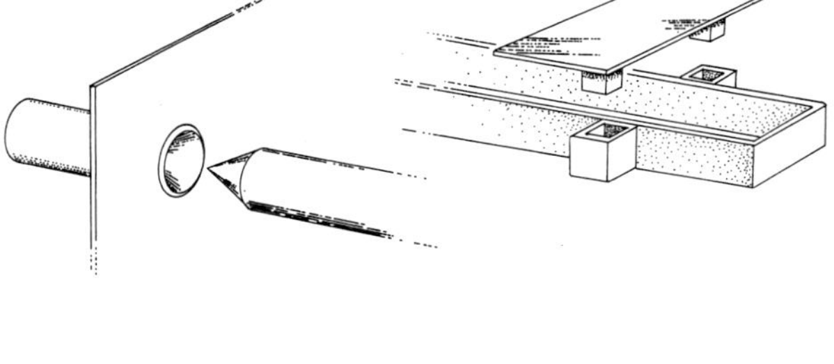

To make a hinge

Cut off the lengths of chenier needed for the knuckles in a jointing tool and also use this tool to file the ends true. To check that the ends of the knuckles are square, stand them on a flat plate against an engineer's square.

File a groove in each side of the article to be hinged to fit the chenier. File a small chamfer on the seam side of the knuckles to take up any excess solder. If solder runs down the groove it will foul the knuckles on the opposite side. Wire the knuckles into place with a hook of steel wire. Interlock them as shown, and ensure they are tight against each other. The wire also keeps the knuckles from being soldered to the wrong side. Solder the knuckles in place, then rivet the hinge.

The position of the chenier in relation to the side determines how the hinge will open. Sometimes a bevel needs to be filed to give clearance. If a chenier with thick walls is used, the knuckles can be filed level with the metal surface to make a neat, flush joint.

► Making chenier fit a rivet. Choose a former the same diameter as the rivet and longer than the chenier. Coat the former with beeswax and pass it straight through the chenier. Lubricate the chenier and pull both through the drawplate. Remove the former by drawing it through a hole too small for the chenier.

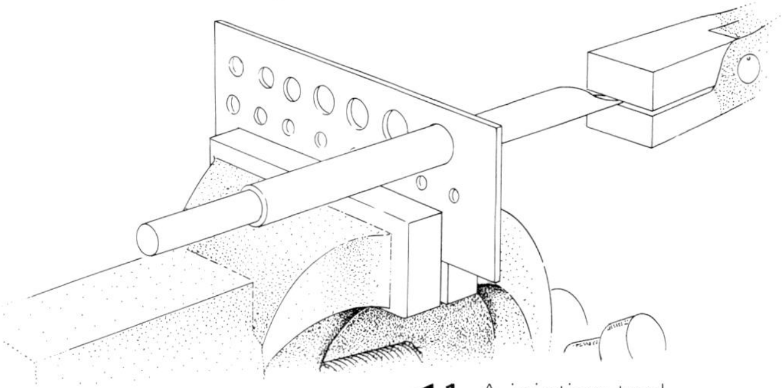

◄ **1.** A jointing tool.
2. Checking knuckles are square.
3. Groove for the hinge.
4. Chamfer on the chenier.
5. Wire on the knuckles and method for interlocking them.
6. The position of the chenier determines the way it opens.
7. Riveting up the hinge.

1

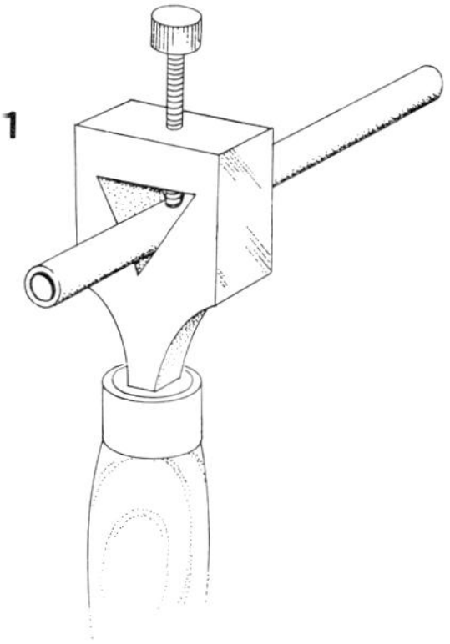

2

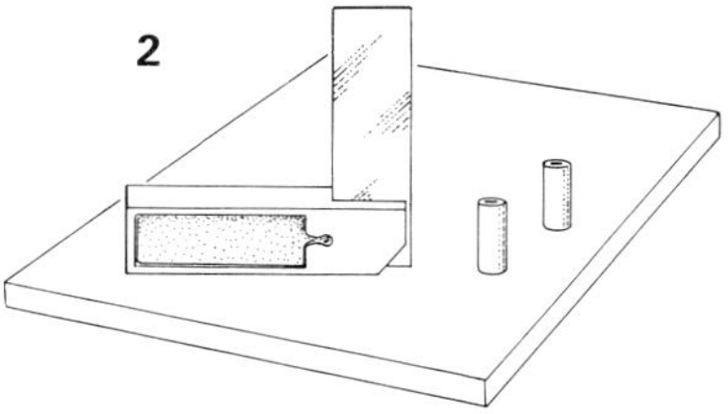

5

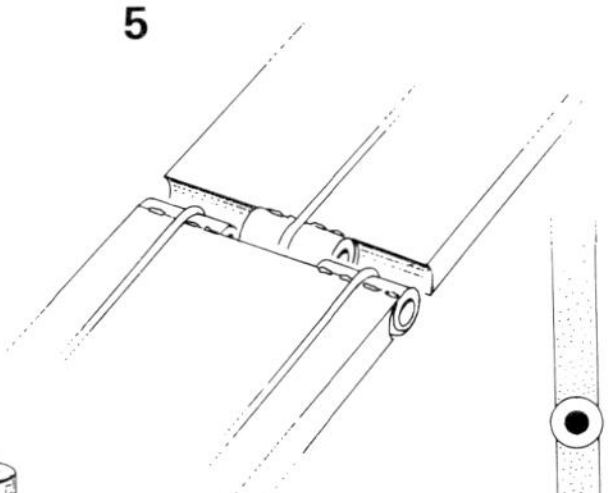

6

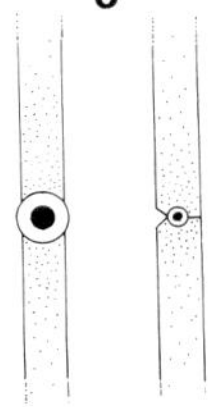

7

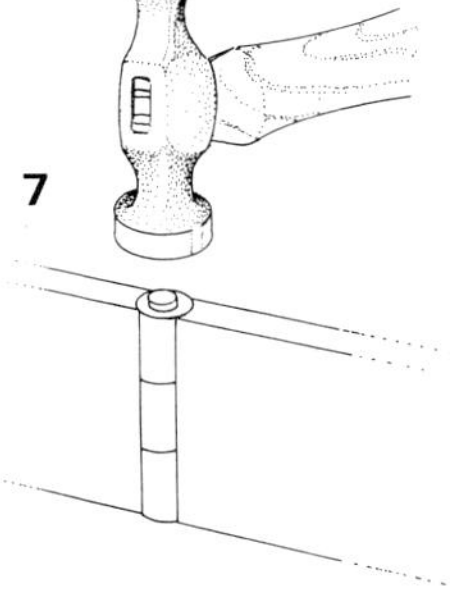

3

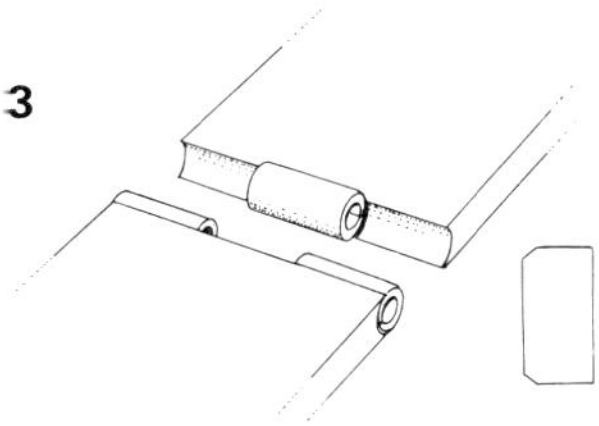

4

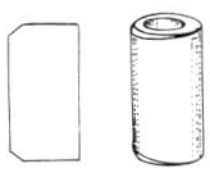

Electro-forming and silver-plating

Electroforming and silverplating are processes in which a layer of metal is deposited on the outside of an article. In silverplating, the surfaces of an object are thinly coated with fine silver. Jewellery is sometimes silverplated to cover fire stain which is difficult to remove. In electroforming, a heavier layer of metal is deposited on a conducting material, either metal, or resin, wax, rubber or glass that is coated with a conducting substance. Originally, electroforming was simply used to reproduce articles but more recently craftsmen, by controlled use of the process, have created original pieces with new and varied surface treatments.

WARNING

Equipment for these processes can be quite simply set up, but the chemicals are dangerous. The cyanide salts used in the plating baths are deadly poisonous and should, therefore, be kept well away from children and animals. Handle the chemicals only with rubber gloves and take care not to splash the skin, clothes, or the bench. Wash thoroughly after using the chemicals. Only use these processes if the working conditions are safe and the operator is confident that the safety precautions are adequate.

◀ Electroformed piece by Stanley Lechtzin, who has carried out much of the recent scientific research into this technique.

Electroforming and silverplating

In both processes, direct current flows through a conducting solution as a stream of charged particles called ions. In silverplating and silver electroforming, silver ions are attracted to the object being coated.

Equipment

For small articles, a dry battery will supply direct current and either pyrex glass beakers or polythene bowls are suitable containers for the solutions. For working, use copper wire to connect the article to the negative terminal of the battery and the fine silver block to the positive terminal. Check the voltage with a voltmeter.

Electroforming

Metal can be deposited on many different materials as long as the surfaces are made conductive. So stones can be set in wax models and the metal formed around them. This is a unique setting process. For electroforming, the same basic techniques as for silverplating are followed, but such things as temperature, solution and voltage are varied for different results. Read further about this technique before beginning.

Silverplating chemicals

The chemicals needed are commercially available. Follow the warnings and instructions carefully. **Silverplating chemicals are dangerous.** The basic process is as follows:

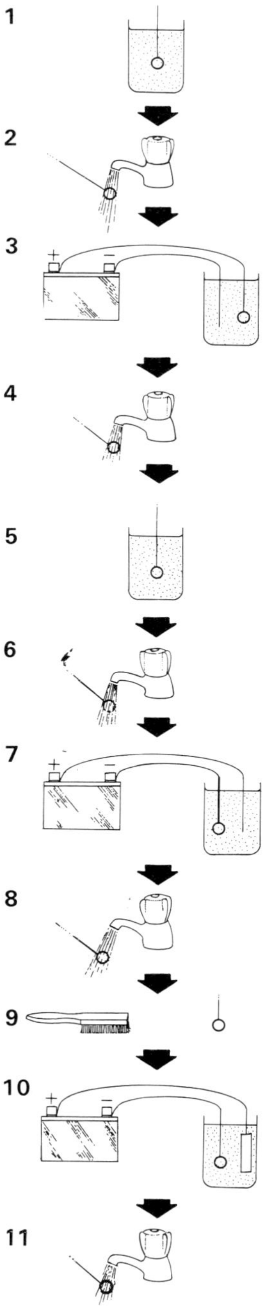

1. Clean off grease with a chemical metal cleaner.

2. Wash thoroughly under cold running water.

3. For electrocleaning, attach the article to the positive terminal, making it the anode and leave it in a cleaning solution for 2–3 minutes at 4–6 volts.

4. Wash thoroughly.

5. Dip in a substance called mercury quickening to provide a covering that helps the adhesion of the silver.

6. Wash thoroughly.

7. Deposit a thin coating of silver (silverstrike) to cover the mercury. Make the article the cathode by attaching it to the negative terminal. Dip in the plating bath for about 15 seconds at 2–4 volts. The anode is 99.9% fine silver.

8. Wash thoroughly.

9. Brush with a brass brush to compress the silverstrike, otherwise staining may occur.

10. For the silver deposit, suspend the article as the cathode in the bath at room temperature. For a heavy deposit leave the article for about 20 minutes at 0.75–1.0 volts.

11. Wash thoroughly.

Cleaning and polishing

Careful finishing is one of the most important stages in the making of jewellery. This process changes rough metalwork into a piece of jewellery. A good finish makes even the simplest article look attractive. It often takes almost as long to clean up and polish jewellery as it does to construct it, but it is well worth spending this time in order to achieve a really high-quality result. In the process of cleaning up, the work marks introduced into the metal during construction are systematically removed. Then, once the surface is completely free of all marks and scratches, it can be polished.

To clean

Pickle to clean off borax and oxide. With a fine file, remove hammer and coarse work marks. Remove all filing lines with a buff stick. For deep depressions, dip a Water of Ayr stone in water and stone off the marks. They will soon disappear and the resulting surface will be fine enough to polish.

How to polish

To polish by hand, glue a piece of suede to a flat stick. Apply the polish to the suede and rub the work. Make an assortment of different sized polishing sticks, including a round one for the insides of rings.

To polish by machine, hold the work in the position shown opposite. Take great care. Tie back long hair and secure loose clothing.

Fire stain

After the first polish, a grey stain may show on the surface of silver. This is cupric oxide, formed when the copper in sterling silver oxidized while the metal was being heated in air. Fire stain is quite thin and can be removed by more filing, buffing or stoning.

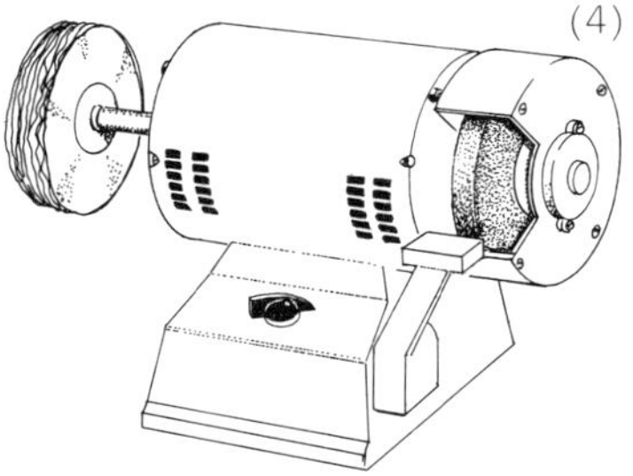

▲ A polishing machine.

▼ Polishing mops: (1) felt; (2) bristle; (3) calico; (4) ring felt.

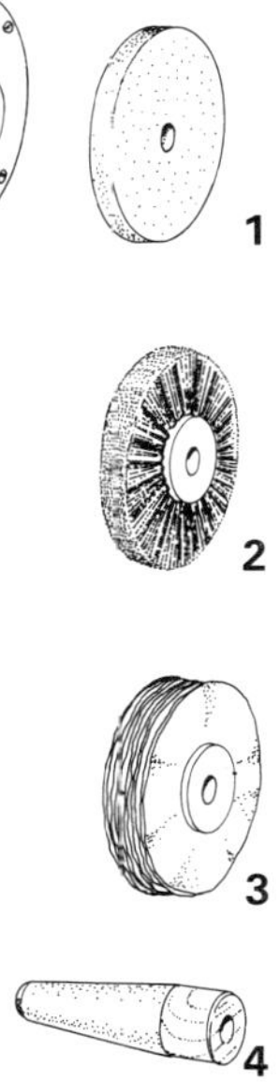

▼ Buff sticks: (1, 2). Polishing compounds: (3) jeweller's rouge; (4) porthos; (5) tripoli; (6) Water of Ayr stone.

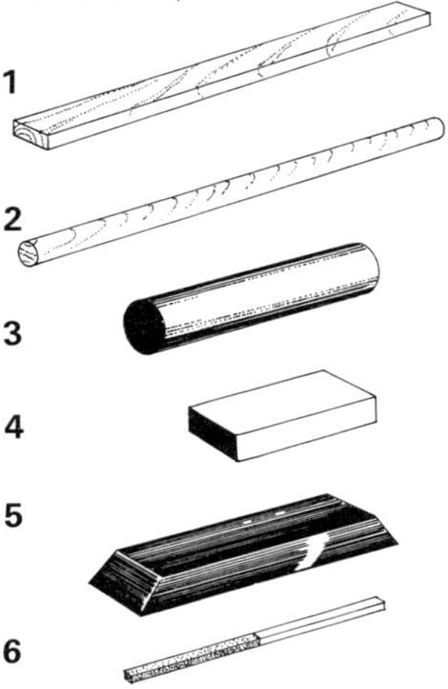

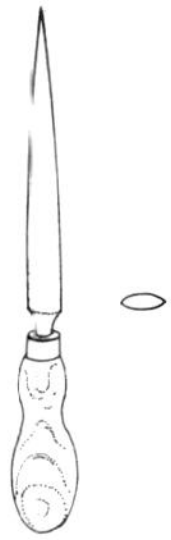

▲ A burnisher.

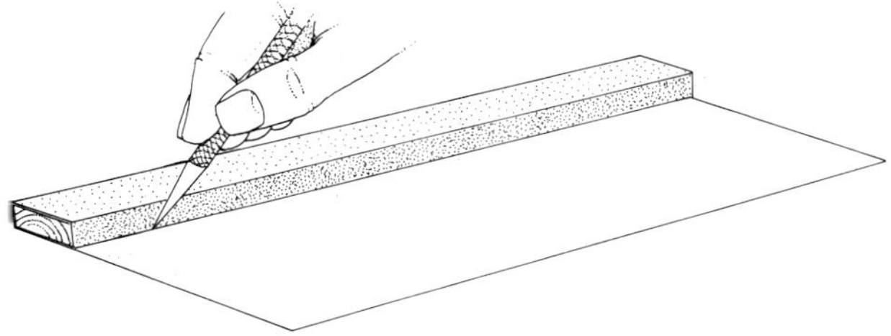

◀ To make a buff stick

Choose a suitably sized stick, 20 cm x 2 cm x 5 mm is convenient, and a flour grade sand paper. Lay the stick on the paper, scribe along the edge of the stick, and bend up the paper. Wrap up the stick tightly.

▶ Abrasives for a pendant drill

Anneal an old drill and saw down the end. Slot in a small piece of sandpaper and wrap it around the drill. Make sure it is wrapped in the correct direction so that it does not unwind when the drill is turned on.

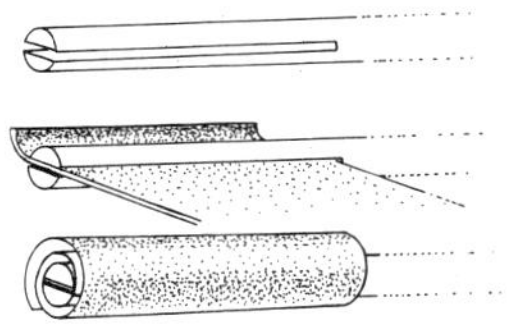

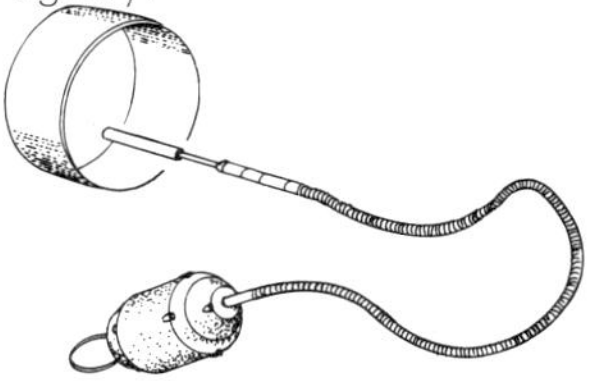

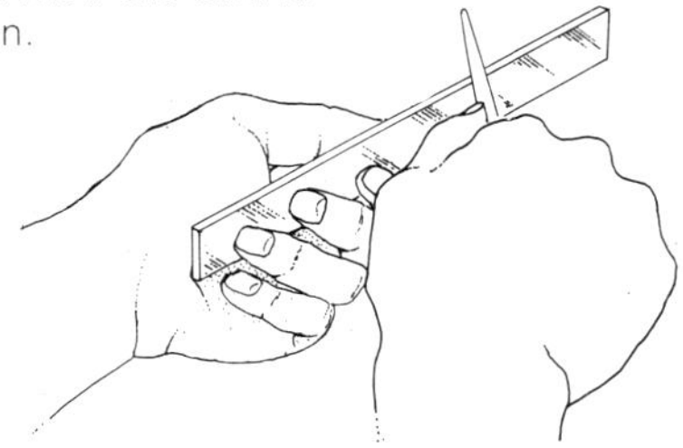

◀ Burnishing

Rub work firmly, but carefully, with a burnisher to smooth and compress the surface. It is often advisable to polish narrow edges in this way to avoid losing sharp corners on the polishing machine.

▶ Polishing

Use porthos or tripoli on felt, bristle and calico mops. Swansdown (soft) mops are for rouge. Polish with tripoli or porthos first, wash the piece well in detergent, then polish with rouge. Wash and dry in box wood shavings or with a soft cloth. Never use the same mop for different abrasives.

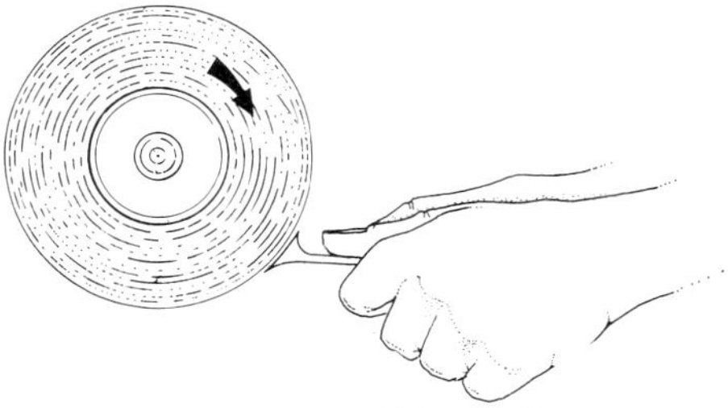

◀ Threading

Polish inside fine holes with polishing threads. Soft string, silk, or even a shoe lace will do. Tie the threads to a convenient hook on the bench, pass them through the hole, apply tripoli or porthos and, holding the threads taut, quickly rub the job up and down the string.

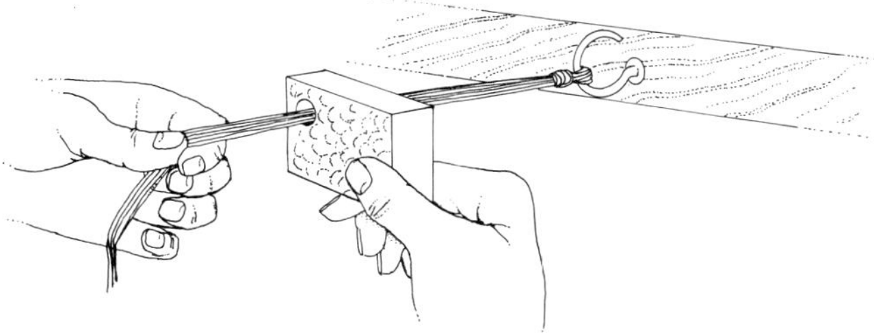

Casting

Casting plays an important part in the mass production of modern jewellery. It can also be used by craftsmen to gain unusual effects. Commercially, lost-wax casting is the most common method used. In this process a model with a 2 mm wire sprue is made in metal. A rubber mould is taken from the model. Wax is then injected into the hole in the rubber. Any number of identical wax patterns can be made from the same rubber. The waxes are all attached to a wax core, which is then surrounded with investment plaster. When this is dry, the wax is burnt out, leaving a hole. Molten metal is forced into the hole with a centrifugal or a vacuum casting machine.

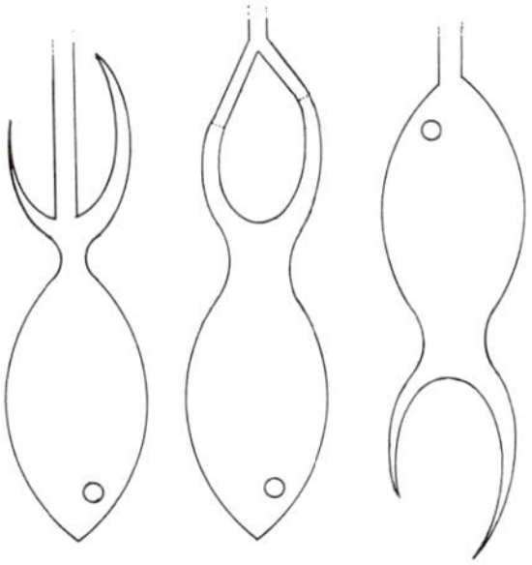

▲ Design for casting.

▼ Stages of casting.
1. Make the model.
2. Take a rubber mould of the model.
3. Inject wax into the mould.
4. Assemble the pieces after they have been cast.

Casting equipment is expensive and conditions need to be carefully controlled. If a design calls for many identical pieces to be cast it is advisable to make up a model and take this to a commercial caster.

Design for casting

Generally, metal will not go up a small hole in the opposite direction to the main flow of metal (see first fish). So either attach a divided sprue to allow molten metal to flow to the mould and open out the bottleneck a little (second fish), or sprue up from the other end (third fish). It is normally better to attach the sprue to the place where the main body of metal will be as this then forms a reservoir to feed the rest of the piece.

When castings come back from the caster, part of the sprue will still be attached. Remove this, then file up the casting as necessary.

When designing for casting, bear in mind that the surface will need to be cleaned up. Either allow easy access for saws and files, or use the cast surface as a texture which can be exaggerated if necessary.

Castings shrink by up to 10%. Check the exact amount with the casting firm chosen and make the model larger as required.

▶ **Cuttlefish casting**
Flatten the surfaces of two pieces of cuttlefish. Put four locating pegs as shown and sandwich the model between the two pieces. Push them together until they meet. Remove the model and make air vents from the depression towards the edge of the cuttlefish. Wire the cuttlefish to a charcoal block that has a carved hollow. Melt scraps of metal in the hollow and tilt the block to pour the molten metal.

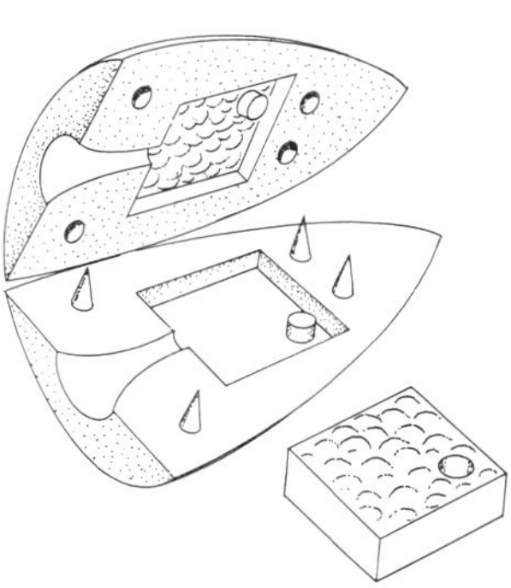

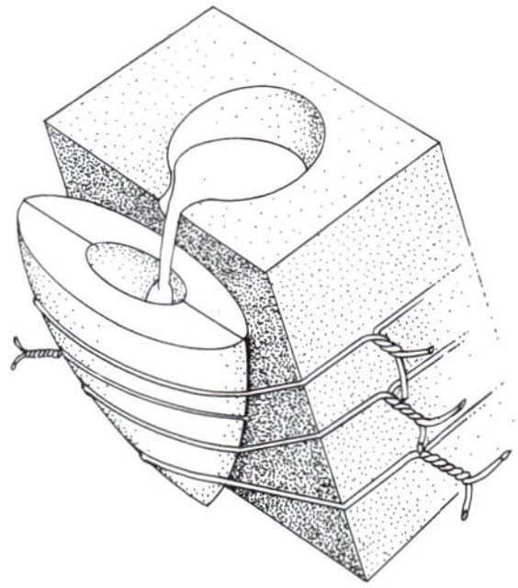

◀ **Charcoal block casting**
Carve a design in a charcoal block. Carve an access channel for the molten metal. Put in four locating pins of wood or metal and push another charcoal block onto the pins until the two touch exactly. Wire them together. Melt the metal in a crucible, and, when the metal is molten and the surface is "rolling", pour it quickly into the opening in the charcoal block. Keep the flame on the metal until the last second to ensure it all pours without solidifying. This casting suits coarse designs only.

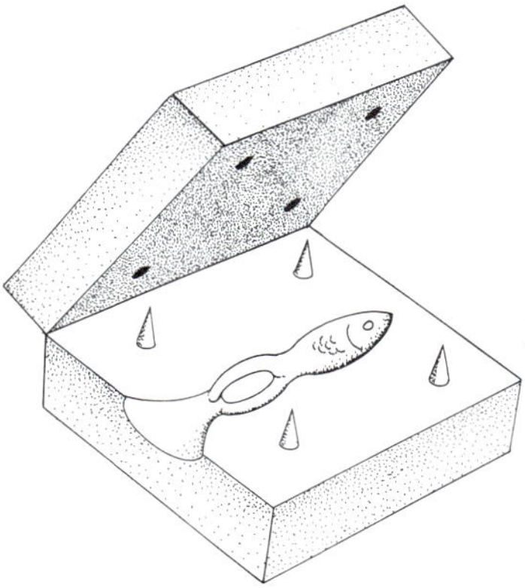

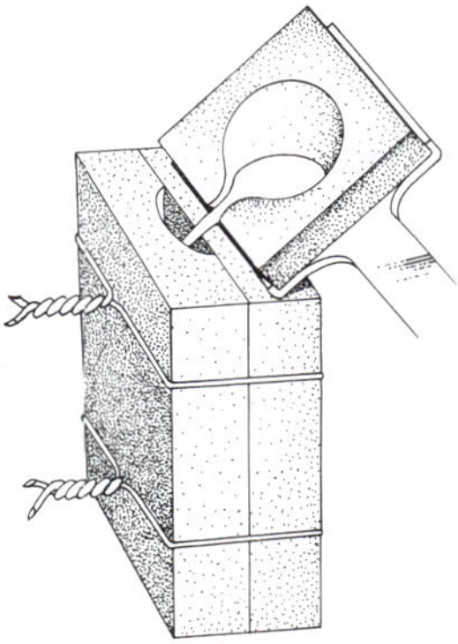

A variety of projects

Jewellery can be made using a few or many of the techniques described previously. Often, simple designs involving uncomplicated processes are the most successful. So begin with easy pieces. As confidence and familiarity with the materials and tools increase, try different ideas. At first, mistakes will be made. These can sometimes be turned to advantage and may lead to new ideas. Usually, the error has to be rectified and the control learned in correcting the mistake is valuable experience. If the error is such that the piece cannot be saved, put it aside. It can be melted with other scraps of the same material and reused.

◀ Fusing
Fusing is a way of joining metal without solder by heating it until the surfaces just begin to melt. This also changes the shape and surface texture of the metal. Try fusing scraps. This will help in learning to recognise the changes in metal during heating.

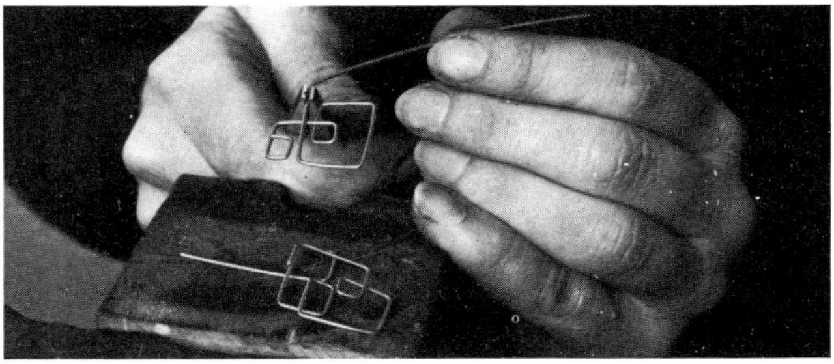

◀ A wire pendant
Bend thin wire with flat-nose pliers. As each corner is bent only once, the metal is not work-hardened so annealing is unnecessary. The ends of the wire are wound together to form the pendant hook, so solder is not needed either.

▶ A simple chain
Begin with a strip of metal of about 8 mm wide and 1.0 mm thick. Cut off lengths of about 25 mm and drill a hole in each end. Twist each piece, using two pairs of pliers. Make wire links to join the twisted lengths. Solder the links. When finished, clean and polish the chain.

To make a hollow ring

Choose a suitable stone. If silver is used, the thickness of metal required is about 1.0 mm for the outside, and 0.8 mm for the liner. If the ring is to be made in gold, the thickness can be reduced slightly as gold is stronger and heavier.

Draft the pattern and transfer it to the metal.

Saw out the outside shape. Anneal the metal. Using half-round pliers, first bend in the ends that will fit around the stone. Then bend up the shank to form the ring. The solder seams are each side of the stone. Adjust the ends to be soldered with a saw or a file until they butt together perfectly. Solder the two side seams with hard solder.

With medium solder, solder in a bearer to support the stone at the correct level. A horizontal bearer (page 56) is easier to fit in this case.

Measure the widest point of the ring. To determine the liner width, add 2 mm to the measurement. Cut a strip of this width from 0.8 mm thick metal and make a ring that fits the finger. Solder with hard solder.

With a half-round hand file, file the inside of the outer ring until the liner fits tightly. Solder the liner in place with easy solder.

Saw away the excess liner, then shape the sides with a file. Filing off the edges of the shank gives a sleek appearance.

With buff sticks remove all file marks and fire stain.

Polish first with tripoli or porthos. If any fire stain remains, remove it. Wash off excess abrasive in detergent, then polish with rouge and wash again.

When thick metal is used, two people may be needed to set the stone. One person taps evenly on the end of a flat-faced punch which the other person moves slowly along the edge of the metal.

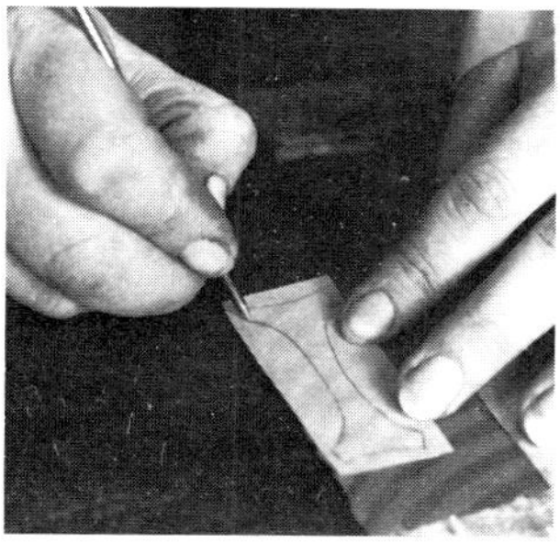

1. Transferring the pattern.

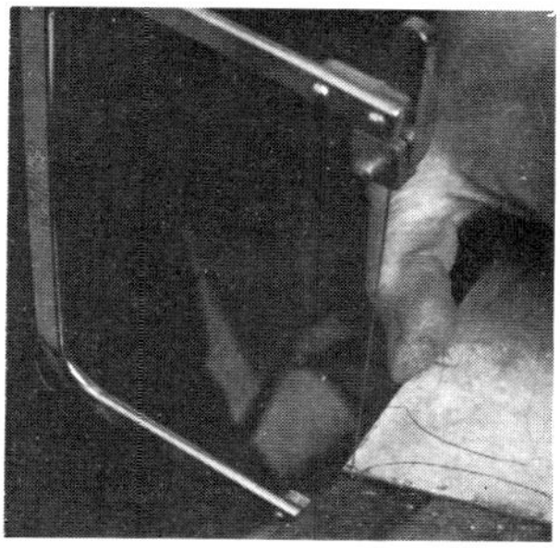

2. Sawing out the metal.

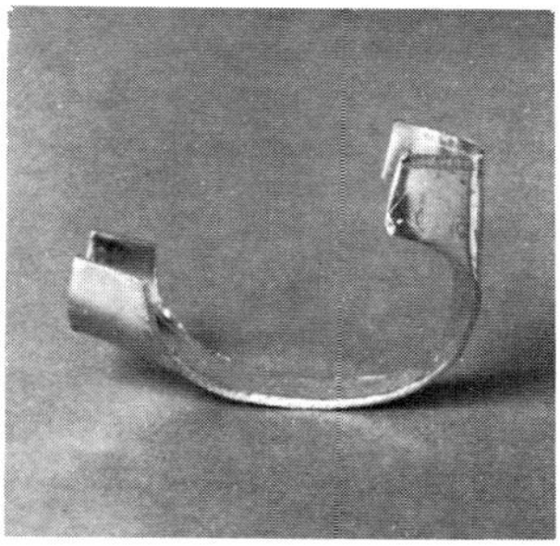

3. Turning up the shape.

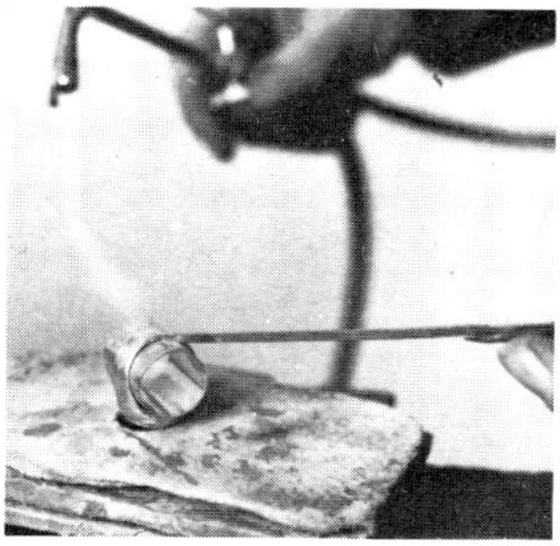

4. Soldering in the liner.

5. Cleaning the ring.

6. Setting the stone.

How to make a built-up ring

The width of the ring and the thickness of the metal can be adjusted within reasonable limits. Metal of 1.2 mm thickness is suitable. Silver less than about 1.0 mm thick would be too weak and metal thicker than about 2.5 mm becomes uncomfortable to wear.

The dimensions of the wire decorations are also a design decision. They should, however, be in keeping with the thickness of the band and the choice of stones. Many fine wires make a delicate decoration, while fewer, heavier wires have a chunky appearance. The wires can be polished or textured.

Other variations can be considered. Taper the band towards the back or round off the edges.

Adjust the positions of the bundles of wires to suit the size of the stone or stones chosen. In this ring, paua shell was filed to suit the design. Because of the shape of the shell, only two claws were needed for each piece of shell. For an oval or round stone, four claws would be necessary. Allowance should be made for clearance of the base of a faceted stone.

◀ The finished pieces

A pendant bent from wire; a fused ring set with a small garnet; a built-up ring with textured wire decoration; a hollow ring set with a malachite and a heavy fused ring.

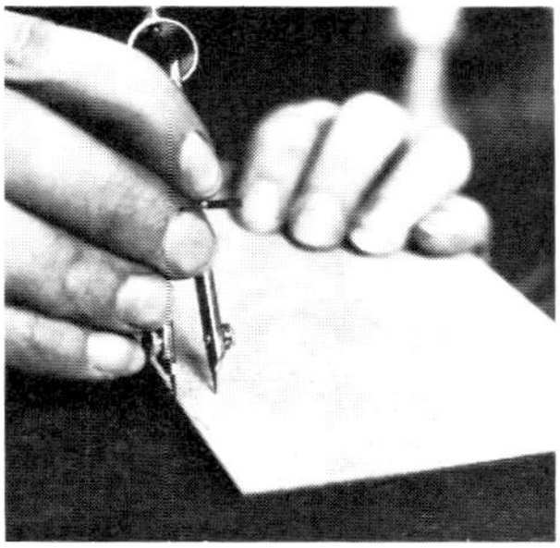

1. Set dividers to the desired width of the ring, say 10 mm. Using a straight edge as a guide, mark the strip.

2. With half-round pliers, bend a circle to fit the finger. Bend the metal very slightly every 2–3 mm. Overlap the ends.

3. Holding the overlapping metal in half-round pliers, saw through both thicknesses to get a closely-fitting joint.

4. Cut 12 mm lengths of wire and hard solder them into triangular bundles, then medium solder the bundles to the ring.

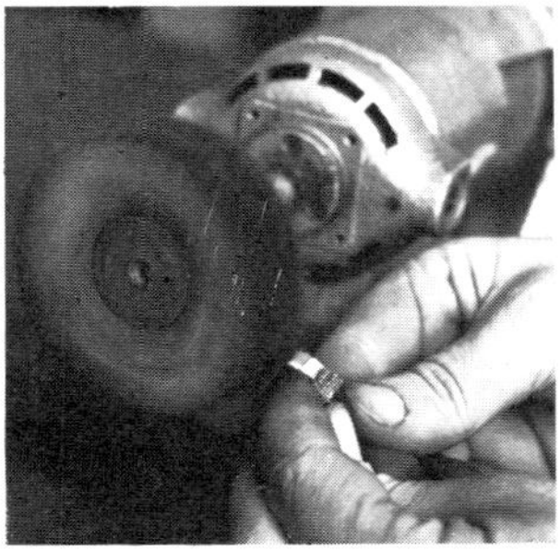

5. Solder on claws using the method on page 44. File the edges level. Polish by hand or by machine. Texture the wires if desired.

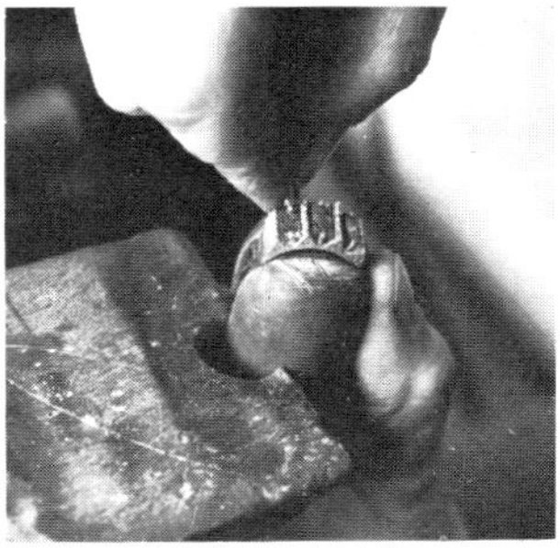

6. Notch out the inside of the claws to fit the girdle of the stone. Taper the outside from the notch to the top. Push over the claw.

Stones

Amber: resin from coniferous trees growing shortly before the great Ice Age has fossilized to form amber. It often contains insects that were trapped when the resin was secreted. Amber is transparent or opaque and ranges in colour from pale yellow to deep brown-red. As it has a very low specific gravity, amber will float in a tumbler ($\frac{1}{3}$ pint) of water in which ten teaspoons of salt have been dissolved. This test distinguishes it from imitations of plastic, bakelite, or perspex which will sink.

Beryl: the most common varieties of beryl are the pale blue to pale blue-green aquamarine and the darker green emerald. Most emeralds contain numerous cracks and inclusions. They are very fragile and break easily. Faultless stones are rare, and a good quality emerald is probably the most expensive of all stones.

Chrysoberyl: the yellow to yellowish-green cabochon stones with a cats-eye effect (chatoyancy) and alexandrite are varieties of chrysoberyl. The colour of alexandrite appears different under different lighting conditions. In daylight it appears green, while under artificial light it looks pinkish-red. Alexandrite is called after Tsar Alexander II as it was discovered in the Urals in 1830 on the day he came of age.

Coral: the pink to dark red coral used in jewellery is made up of numerous skeletons of coral polypi. The colonies of corals mass together into tree-shaped formations. Coral is relatively soft and so can be carved using techniques similar to those used for ivory. It is often imitated by plastic, but can be tested by touching the surface with a small drop of acid. Coral effervesces in contact with acid, plastic does not.

Corundum: the most common varieties of corundum are the red ruby and the blue sapphire. The colour of ruby ranges from pale pink to deep red. The most highly rated colour is the dark red with a tinge of purple known as pigeon's blood. The blue of sapphire also varies from a pale colour, through the highly esteemed cornflower-blue, to a dark velvet-blue. Corundum can be produced synthetically. Under a lens which magnifies ten times (10x) synthetic stones can normally be distinguished from natural stones. Small air bubbles or clouds of unfused powder can often be seen in synthetic stones, whereas natural stones have natural inclusions such as lines like threads of silk or feathers.

Diamond: the diamond is probably the stone most frequently set into jewellery. Although it is the hardest stone, its crystal properties are such that it will split (cleave) easily if hit in a particular way. One legend tells of a dealer who, many years ago, "tested" stones by hammering them. Stones that broke were pronounced worthless and the finder was not paid. However the cleaved sections could still be polished for use in jewellery. The diamond exhibits typical flashes of colour known as fire and this

Cuts of Stones

BRILLIANT CUT

Top

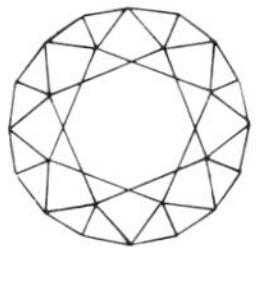

Side

Base

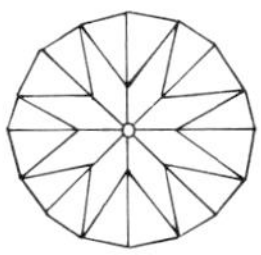

ROSE CUT

Top

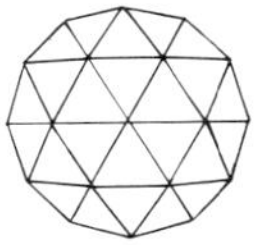

Side

EIGHT CUT

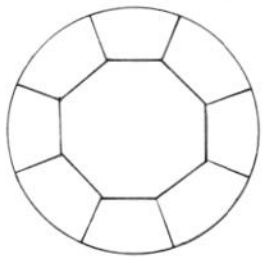

SWISS CUT

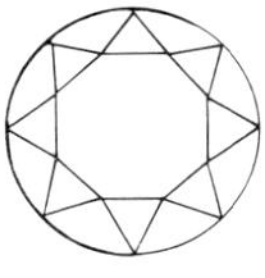

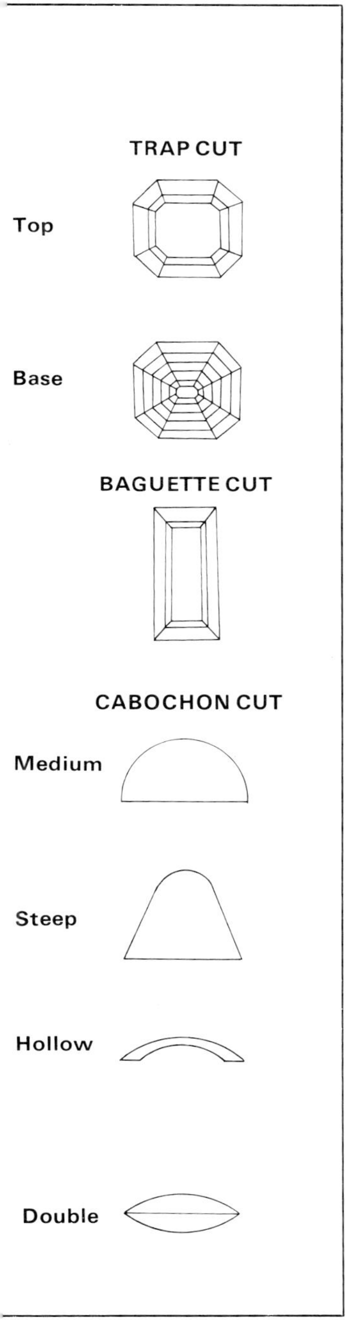

helps to distinguish it from some substitutes. Also diamonds found in jewellery are rarely totally without fault. They frequently have small characteristic black or white marks.

Garnet: there are several varieties of garnet used in jewellery.
Hessonite—yellow-red to golden colour.
Pyrope—blood-red colour. The stones are usually small, but are free from faults.
Almandine—deep red tinged with purple. This is the stone sometimes cut into a cabochon and called a carbuncle.
Demantoid—dark green to yellowish green.

Ivory: ivory comes from the tusks of the elephant, rhinoceros, hippopotamus, and walrus, and the teeth of the hippopotamus and the narwhal. Colour and markings vary according to the source of the material. Being a soft substance, it is easily carved and polished for use in jewellery. To distinguish real ivory from substitutes, heat a small scraping in a test tube and check the fumes with red litmus paper. The fumes from ivory are alkaline so, if the scrapings are genuine, the litmus paper will turn blue.

Jade: the term jade refers to two different stones.
Nephrite—varies in colour from white to dark green. The Maoris in New Zealand used nephrite from early times to carve ornaments, weapons, and jewellery.
Jadeite—found in a variety of colours including white, green, brown, red, mauve. This material is highly valued by the Chinese who carve it into ornaments of all colours.

Jet: jet, the fossilized wood of a coniferous tree, is soft and takes a high polish. It was most popular in the last century when it was set into fashionable mourning jewellery. A hot needle touched to the jet will produce the smell of burning coal, so it can be distinguished from stone and synthetic substitutes.

Lapis lazuli: lapis lazuli is an even dark blue in colour. It is frequently flecked with glistening yellow flakes of iron pyrites. As it is almost opaque and has a poor lustre, it is not faceted.

Malachite: malachite is found in all shades of green. The colours follow a characteristic banded pattern and the stone is cut cabochon to show the banding to best advantage. A drop of acid will cause the malachite to effervesce so genuine malachite can be distinguished from substitutes.

Opal: opal is a solidified non-crystalline jelly. The characteristic opalescent flashes of colour result from interference of light rays by small particles of silica. It is a soft material and easily damaged so it is often made into triplets. First there is a layer of potch (rough opal), then a thin layer of coloured opal, and the top is protected by a cabochon shaped quartz crystal. The three layers are clearly seen from the side of the stone. Until the early nineteenth century the opal was considered a lucky stone. But the novel, "Anne of Geierstein" by Sir Walter Scott changed this. In the story, Lady Hermione wore an opal which changed colour according to her moods. One day she became unconscious, and,

Amber
Diamond
Chrysoberyl
Beryl
Jade
Alexandrite (Chrysoberyl)
Ruby (Corundum)
Aquamarine (Beryl)
Emerald (Beryl)
Beryl
Quartz
Sapphire (Corundum)
Lapis Lazuli
Amethyst
Ivory & Jet
Malachite

Turquoise
Tourmaline
Zircon
Coral
Garnet
Coral
Topaz
Pearl
Spinel
Tigers Eye
Peridot
Opal
Cornelian
Agate

during her maid's short absence from her room, both Lady Hermione and the opal disappeared. Only a small pile of ashes remained. The opal was Queen Victoria's favourite stone and she gave them as presents to her daughters. This however did not dispel the popular aversion to the stone.

Pearl: a pearl is formed if an irritant such as a piece of sand or broken shell intrudes into the shell of certain bivalve molluscs. The mollusc covers the irritant with overlapping layers of nacre which produce the characteristic sheen. Pearls can be cultivated, called cultured pearls, by inserting a small bead into the mollusc. When the bead is removed after several years it is coated with nacreous layers. Specialized equipment is needed to determine the difference between natural and cultured pearls. A simple test to distinguish glass imitations is to rub the material over the teeth. A real or cultured pearl feels "gritty", glass imitations feel smooth.

Peridot: peridot is found coloured yellow, green-yellow, dark green, light green and brown. In its cut form, peridot can be distinguished from other green stones by its oily appearance.

Quartz: quartz occurs in large quantities all over the world. It can be divided into crystalline and cryptocrystalline varieties. Crystalline—some of the common varieties are:

amethyst	purple
citrine	yellow
rose quartz	pink
cairngorm	yellow to red-brown
smoky quartz	brown
tigers eye	yellow chatoyant
rock crystal	colourless

Cryptocrystalline—varieties, called calcedony, are:

cornelian	translucent red
bloodstone	dark green with patches of red jasper
agate	varieties of browns and greys
onyx	dark to black
jasper	red to brown

Spinel: spinel occurs naturally in purples, blues, greens, reds, and black. It is made synthetically in a wide variety of colours to imitate other more expensive stones. The synthetic stones usually have inclusions typical of the verneuile process by which they are made. That is, trapped air bubbles and patches of undissolved powder.

Topaz: the yellow and brown varieties of topaz are the most common although it may also be colourless or blue to green. The red or pink varieties rarely occur naturally but are normally heat treated brown stones.

Tourmaline: this is one of the few stones in jewellery which is sometimes set as a natural crystal, or a slice from a natural crystal. The crystal has a roughly triangular cross section and the sides are deeply striated. The colours found are red, blue, green, and yellow and some crystals exhibit all colours.

Turquoise: turquoise is valued for its colour which can be blue or green. It has a waxy lustre and is difficult to distinguish from the many imitations. Turquoise matrix has patches of turquoise and dark brown or black patches of limonite.

Zircon: zircon has a lustre almost as bright as diamond. It can be identified by its strong double refraction. That is, if the edges of the back facets are viewed through the table facet, the edges appear as double lines. Zircon occurs naturally in a number of different colours, but the colour of the stones used in jewellery is usually the result of heat treatment.

HARDNESS OF STONES

The hardness is given by a figure from 0 to 10 on Mohs' scale. It is not a quantitative measure but gives some indication of the relative hardness of stones.

Stone	Hardness
Amber	2–2½
Beryl—Aquamarine	7½–8
Emerald	7½–8
Coral	3½
Corundum	9
Chrysoberyl	8½
Diamond	10
Garnet—Hessonite	6½–7
Pyrope	7¼
Demantoid	6½
Almandine	7½
Ivory	2–3
Jade—Jadeite	6½–7
Nephrite	6–6½
Jet	3½
Lapis Lazuli	5½
Malachite	3½
Opal	5–6½
Pearl	2½–3½
Peridot	6½–7
Quartz	7
Spinel	8
Topaz (yellow, pink)	8
Tourmaline	7–7½
Turquoise	6
Zircon	7½

Useful tables

Acids for etching

ETCHING ACIDS ARE DANGEROUS. Store them in a labelled glass-stoppered bottle. When mixing, always add acid to water. Etch in a glass dish.

For silver: 3 parts of water, 1 part of concentrated nitric acid.

For gold .375 (9 ct), .585 (14 ct): 50 parts of water, 1 part iron perchloride, 8 parts concentrated hydrochloric acid, 4 parts concentrated nitric acid.

Melting Points & Specific Gravities of Metals

Metal	Melting point °C	Specific gravity
Platinum	1773	21.4
Gold		
fine	1063	19.36
.916 (22 ct)	1003	17.7
.750 (18 ct)	905	15.58
.585 (14 ct)	838	13.4
.375 (9 ct)	830	11.3
Silver		
fine	961	10.53
sterling	893	10.4
Copper	1083	8.94
Brass	940	8.5
Silver solder		
Enamelling	800	
Hard	778	
Medium	765	
Easy	723	

N.B. the melting points of solder are different for each manufacturer, these figures are a guide. Bullion was once measured in Troy ounces but is now measured in gms.

1 Troy ounce = 31.104 gms.

Calculating costs

If a piece already made up is to be copied in another metal, the cost can be calculated as follows. Weigh the piece, then use the table on the left to find the specific gravities (S.G.) of the two metals. The weight of the copy will be given by the formula:

$$\frac{\text{weight of original} \times \text{S.G. of copy}}{\text{S.G. of original}}$$

To get the cost, multiply by the cost per gramme of the metal.

Recipes for Niello

Recipe by	Pliny	Theophilus	Henrich
	Parts	Parts	Parts
Silver	3	2	1
Copper	1	1	2
Sulphur	2	some	6
Lead	0	$\frac{1}{2}$	3

Weights of metals of specified thickness

Thickness of metal mm	Thickness of metal inch	nearest BMG	Sheet: Weight in g. per cm² st. silver	Sheet: 9 ct gold	Sheet: 18 ct gold	Round Wire: Weight in g. per metre st. silver	Round Wire: 9 ct gold	Round Wire: 18 ct gold
0.30	0.012	4	0.31	0.34	0.47	0.73	0.80	1.10
0.40	0.016	6	0.42	0.45	0.62	1.29	1.42	1.96
0.55	0.022	8	0.57	0.62	0.87	2.44	2.68	3.70
0.70	0.028	10	0.73	0.79	1.09	3.95	4.35	6.00
0.90	0.035	12	0.94	1.02	1.40	6.53	7.19	9.91
1.10	0.043	14	1.14	1.24	1.71	10.48	10.74	14.81
1.30	0.051	16	1.35	1.47	2.03	13.63	15.00	20.68
1.50	0.059	18	1.56	1.70	2.34	18.15	19.97	27.54
1.65	0.065	20	1.72	1.86	2.57	24.70	27.18	37.48
2.10	0.083	24	2.18	2.37	3.27	72.59	79.89	110.14
3.20	0.126	28	3.33	3.62	4.99	82.59	90.89	125.32

STANDARD MARK
British Articles

Before 1975	Standard	From 1975
	22 carat gold Marked in England Marked in Scotland	
	18 carat gold Marked in England Marked in Scotland	
14 585	14 carat gold	
9 375	9 carat gold	
	Sterling silver Marked in England Marked in Scotland	
	Britannia silver	
—	Platinum	

Imported Articles

Before 1975	Standard	From 1975
22 ·916	22 carat gold	916
18 ·750	18 carat gold	750
14 ·585	14 carat gold	585
9 ·375	9 carat gold	375
·925	Sterling silver	925
·9584	Britannia silver	958
—	platinum	950

ASSAY OFFICE MARK
British Articles

Before 1975		From 1975
 gold & St. silver / Brit. silver	**London**	 gold, silver & platinum
 gold / silver	**Birming-ham**	 gold & silver platinum
 gold / silver	**Sheffield**	 gold, silver & platinum
 gold & silver	**Edinburgh**	 gold & silver

Imported Articles

Before 1975		From 1975
gold / silver 	**London**	gold & silver same / platinum 
	**Birming-ham**	same 
	**Sheffield**	same —
	**Edinburgh**	same —

DATE LETTERS—examples

London		Edinburgh
p	1970	P
q	1971	Q
r	1972	R
s	1973	
t	1974	S
A	1975	A
B	1976	B
C	1977	C

COMPLETE MARKS examples

Britannia silver made in UK by Nathaniel Lock, marked in London in 1705-6.

Sterling silver made in UK by Robert Bowman, marked in Edinburgh in 1780-1.

Eighteen-carat gold made in UK by NM, marked in London in 1952-3.

Nine-carat gold made abroad, imported by NM, marked in Glasgow in 1952-3.

Twenty-two-carat gold made in UK by NM, marked in Sheffield in 1952-3.

Sterling silver made in UK by NM, marked in Edinburgh in 1935 with special mark commemorating the silver jubilee of King George V and Queen Mary.

Hall-marking

A hallmark is a form of quality control. Roman and Byzantine articles have been found with marks which were probably a type of hallmark, but it was not until 1238 that hallmarks were legally required in England. Later, other countries introduced marking systems.

The English hallmark is internationally recognised and respected because, from its first introduction, it has been carefully supervised. The first hallmark was initiated by Henry III when substandard silverware was sold to the court. Henry ordered that six 'discreet' silversmiths from the powerful silversmiths' guild in London be made responsible for the quality of the silver in the work produced by other members of the guild. The six were called wardens and today, there are still wardens at the Worshipful Company of Goldsmiths.

Initially the standard for silver had to be 11 ozs troy 2 pennyweights of silver to every 12 ozs troy of metal. This was the same standard as the coinage and was called sterling silver. For gold, the standard had to be 'no worse gold than the Touch of Paris' which was $19\frac{1}{5}$ parts of gold in every 24 parts of metal, or $19\frac{1}{5}$ carats. It was also specified that no article was to leave the worker's hands until one of the wardens had tested it (assayed it) and stamped it with a leopard's head to show that the piece had passed the test.

In the early 1400's a law was introduced which stated that no 'workmanship of silver' could be 'set to sale' in London unless it was marked with the identifying mark of the craftsman as well as the leopard's head. Also that century, a letter to indicate the year the article was assayed, was added to the maker's mark and the leopard's head. This was primarily to reduce the possibilities of corruption of the staff in the Assay Office as a date letter meant that an article could be linked with the person responsible for the assay.

By the 1500's the guild had become the Goldsmiths' Company and it was empowered to fine or send to prison any craftsman who tried to pass off substandard wares. Poor quality goods were confiscated. Today the Assay Office still breaks a piece made from metal that falls below the specified standards. This prevents the piece being fraudulently offered for sale.

In 1544 Henry VIII reduced the standard of metal used in coinage. The standards for silver in wrought work were retained at their original levels, so a lion passant guardant was added as a guarantee to clients of the quality of the metal.

And so the hallmark recognised today was established.

In the late seventeenth century there was an increased demand for silver plate. To satisfy the needs for silver, craftsmen melted down old coinage, which led to a shortage of sterling silver for the new coinage being minted at the time. So a statute was introduced that raised the standard required for wrought work to 11 ozs troy 10 pennyweights of silver to every 12 ozs troy of metal. This was known as Britannia Standard and two new compulsory marks were added to the hallmark to indicate the standard.

At various times during the eighteenth century duty was payable on silver. The amount was calculated on the weight of the metal in the article and collected at the time of assay. This led to various malpractices on the part of craftsmen who tried to avoid the duty. Either an old hallmark was removed from plate about to be remelted and soldered to the new piece, or the work sent to the assay office was only a small part of the complete article.

Gradually, as craftsmen began to group in other parts of the country, new Assay offices were established. There was some opposition to this from the Goldsmiths' Company who feared a fall in standards. A great deal of controversy surrounded the setting up of the offices at Birmingham and Sheffield and extensive political pressure was applied before the bill establishing the offices was passed through Parliament. Traditionally new offices took their marks from the town's coat of arms, but, in this case, the marks were drawn from the Crown and Anchor pub in the Strand where much of the political discussion occurred. Sheffield took the crown and Birmingham the anchor.

The gradual movement of craftsmen led to some offices being less and less used and so as demand for hallmarking decreased in an area, the Assay Office was shut.

Today London, Birmingham, Sheffield and Edinburgh are the Assay Offices open and, on application they will forward information about hallmarks and registering a mark.

The publishers would like to acknowledge the help of the Assay Offices of Great Britain in providing information for the illustrated marks.

Suppliers

Many of the simple tools needed in working on jewellery can be purchased at a good ironmongers, or can even be contrived from other old tools. DIY shops and general art and craft shops are also worth trying for tools and supplies, and may be willing to order what you need. Some specialist suppliers are listed below. On request they will send a catalogue of equipment which is available.

Charles Cooper Ltd.,
Wall House,
12 Hatton Wall,
Hatton Garden,
London EC1N 8JQ.
01-405 6083

Frank Pike,
58g Hatton Garden,
London EC1N 8LX.
01-405 2688

H. S. & S. Walsh Ltd.,
243 Beckenham Road,
Beckenham.
and at:
11–16 Clerkenwell Road,
London EC1.

R. J. Edwards & Sons,
93–95 Barr Street,
Birmingham 19.

S. Lanzetter,
36 New Brown Street,
Manchester.

George Panton & Sons,
Buchanan Street,
Glasgow.

For supplies of silver sheet, wire, strip and tube in fairly small quantities:

Johnson Matthey Metals,
43 Hatton Garden,
London EC1.
01-405 6959
and at:
Vittoria Street,
Birmingham B1 3NZ.
021-236 9811
and:
175 Arundel Gate,
Sheffield S1 1JY.
0742-23121

Blundell's,
199 Wardour Street,
London W1.
01-437 4746

For copper sheet or wire:

J. Smith & Sons,
42 St. John Square,
London EC1.
01-253 1277
Copper pipe can be bought from a plumbers' merchant. Other metals can often be obtained in the form of offcuts from commercial stockists whose names can be found in the Yellow Pages. Electroplaters can also be found there.

Semi-precious stones are supplied by stockists throughout the country, many of which advertise in "Gem Craft" magazine published monthly price 30p, and "Gems" a bi-monthly at the same price, both obtainable through newsagents. Most lapidary dealers also supply jewellers' findings.

Courses

Local education authorities throughout the country run jewellery courses during the day and in the evening. Many of these are for absolute beginners but others are at a more advanced level. Public demand for these courses is increasing and each year sees an expansion in the number offered. For information contact your local education authority, or local college. Public libraries also carry information about courses in their area. In London the publication "Floodlight", which lists evening classes offered in the ILEA area and covers jewellery courses, is obtainable from newsagents. At a higher level jewellery can be studied as a vocational course at various colleges throughout the country. These courses cover the various aspects of the subject, particularly design. Colleges should be approached direct for their prospectus. To discover which colleges offer courses, and the general qualifications offered, contact should be made with the relevant Regional Advisory Council for Further Education. These Councils are constituted in ten areas covering the whole of the country. For brevity they are listed here under area, location and telephone number. Each carries lists of courses in the area concerned.

London: 01-308 0027

East Anglia (Norwich): 0603-611122 Ext. 5072

East Midlands (Nottingham): 0602-293291

Northern (Newcastle): 0632-81 3212

North Western (Manchester): 061-236 5357

Southern (Reading): 0734-52120

South West (Taunton): 0823-85491

West Midlands (Birmingham): 021-235-2628

Yorkshire & Humberside (Leeds): 0532-40751

Wales (Cardiff): 0222-561231

Book list

There are a number of books available on the different aspects of jewellery. Public libraries tend to have a good selection of books, but with the growing interest in the subject these tend to be out on loan, particularly during the winter period.

CRAFT

Design & Creation of Jewellery, Von Neumann, Pitman, 1973, £8.50.

Contemporary Jewellery: A Studio Handbook, P. Morton, Holt-Blond, 1976, £13.25.

Simple Craft Jewellery, C. G. Dechaume, Faber, 1964, £1.95.

Modern Jewellery—Design & Techniques, I. Brynner, Van Nostrand Reinhold, 1968, £4.50.

Ideas for Jewellery, I. Davidson, Batsford, 1973, £3.35.

Metal Techniques for Craftsmen, O. Cuntracht, Robert Hale, 1969, £12.50.

HISTORY

A History of Jewels, J. A. Black, Orbis, 1974, £12.50.

Art of Jewellery, G. Hughes, Studio Vista, 1972, £8.00.

Jewellery through the Ages, G. Gregorietti, Paul Hamlyn, 1969, £3.50.

GEMMOLOGY

Practical Gemmology, R. Webster, NAG Press, 1967, £3.50.

Gemmologists' Compendium, R. Webster, NAG Press, 1964, £3.25.

HALLMARKING

Book of Hall Marks, Bradbury, Northend, 1975, £3.60 & 96p.

Hall Marks on English Silver, Bly, Shire Publications, 1974, 60p.

DICTIONARY

An Illustrated Dictionary of Jewellery, A. Mason & D. Parker, Osprey Publishing, 1973, £5.95.

Glossary

Anneal: heat metal to red heat, or any suitable temperature, and cool it. This process improves the malleability and softness of a metal after it has been hardened by working.
Asbestos: a non-flammable fibrous material sometimes used for soldering on. Asbestos dust is now considered dangerous. Synthetic soldering blocks are available as an alternative.
Assay: a test to determine the exact quantity of gold, silver, or platinum in a sample of metal.
Baguette: a precious stone cut into a small rectangular shape.
Baroque pearl: an unevenly shaped pearl.
Base metal: common metal which is subject to corrosion e.g. copper, iron, nickel, tin.
Binding wire: steel wire used to tie pieces of metal together for soldering.
Boracic acid: to prevent fire stain. It is mixed to a paste with methylated spirits and coated all over the silver to stop air getting to the surface during heating.
Borax: a flux. When heated it fuses to form a glass-like substance that dissolves the metallic oxides. The surface is then clean for soldering.
Bunsen burner: a small upright gas burner.
Cameo: originally a relief design cut into hard stone such as banded chalcedony. The relief design is carved into the lighter stone, leaving the darker material as a background. Cameos are now also cut into shell.
Carat: 1. Unit of weight. The original carat is thought to have been equal to one seed of a locust tree and was probably used by Eastern pearl traders. The metric carat now used is equal to one fifth of a gram.
2. A measure of fineness of gold. Fine gold or pure gold is equal to 24 carats. So 22 carat gold means 22 parts in 24 of gold, the remaining two parts being metals such as silver or copper. Similarly 18 ct, 14 ct, and 9 ct refer to the number of parts of gold in every 24 parts of metal.
Chasing: punching a relief design into metal from the front.
Chatelaine: an ornament clipped to the belt. Useful household objects such as watches, scissors, seals were hung from it.
Claw setting: a method for holding stones in which a number of wires or claws are used. This type of setting allows light to the back of the stone and is therefore suitable for faceted stones.
Collet: the metal which surrounds and supports a stone.
Diadem: a head ornament.
Drawplate: a steel plate with graded holes. Wire is decreased in diameter or changed in cross-sectional shape by pulling (drawing) it through a drawplate.
Ductile: the property of a metal that enables it to withstand reshaping or stretching.
Electroforming: the process of forming shapes by depositing a heavy layer of metal on a conductive surface.
Electroplating: the depositing of a thin coat of metal on a metal surface.
Electrum: a naturally occurring alloy of gold and silver.
Emery paper: an abrasive which is glued to a paper backing. Various grades of abrasive are available.
Engraving: cutting into metal with a sharp steel tool (graver).
Etching: the controlled use of acid to corrode metal.
Facet: a flat face polished onto a gemstone.
Faience: glazed earthenware or porcelain used to imitate stones.
Ferrous metal: any metal containing iron.
Fibula: a primitive form of brooch.
Filigree: a decoration of thin flattened wires stood on edge to form patterns.
Findings: the catches, joints and clips that make the ornament wearable as jewellery.
Firestain: the dark grey layer of copper oxide that forms on the surface of sterling silver when it is heated in air.
Flux: a substance used in soldering to prevent oxide forming around the area to be soldered. Oxide inhibits the flow of solder.
Forging: the process of hammering metal to change its shape.
Fusing: the process of joining by melting.
Gallery: decorated strip metal used as a border.
Gilding: the covering of a material with a thin layer of gold.
Gilding metal: an alloy of copper and zinc. It is used in jewellery which is to be gilded as it has a similar colour to gold.
Gold: the most ductile and malleable metal. Pure gold is quite soft. It is normally alloyed with other metals for use in jewellery.
Granulation: the application of numerous tiny balls to form a pattern.
Hallmark: a mark stamped on articles to show that the quality of metal used has been tested and found to be of the standard required. The hallmark consists of:
(1) sponsor's mark to indicate the person responsible for the article,
(2) Assay Office mark to identify

the authority that tested the article,
(3) quality mark to guarantee that the metal is of the quality specified,
(4) date letter to show the year the article was stamped.
Hardness: the ability of a metal to resist scratching or abrasion.
Ingot: a cast bar of metal.
Inlay: the process of embedding one material into another so that all surfaces are level.
Intaglio: a design carved into the surface of a material. When the carved depression is pressed into soft wax, a raised pattern is produced.
Lapidary: the art of cutting and polishing gemstones.
Line tool: a steel graver that will cut many parallel lines at one time.
Malleable: a metal is malleable if it is easily extended in all directions by hammering or rolling.
Mandrel: a wood or metal shape which can be used many times to form metal, e.g. the links of a chain are wound around a mandrel.
Marcasites: (iron pyrites): stones with a high metallic lustre. They are usually cut into low six-sided pyramids with a flat base.
Marquise: an oval shape, but pointed at each end.
Matrix: a combination of precious stone and rock in which the stone is deposited, e.g. turquoise matrix.
Mill: (hand rolling mill): steel rollers similar to an old clothes mangle. It is used for reducing the thickness of metal.
Mohs' scale of hardness: used to determine the hardness of gemstones. A mineral will scratch one with a lower number on the scale, but will not scratch one with a higher number. The divisions between numbers are not equal.
Nickel silver (German silver): an alloy of copper, nickel and zinc. It contains no silver. It is often used in costume jewellery or for articles to be silver plated.
Niello: a metal and sulphur mixture which can be fused into depressions in metal to create a blue-black decoration.
Nugget: a lump of metal in its natural state.
Opus interrasile: an open design cut into a sheet of metal with a chisel.
Parure: a matching suite of jewels. It might include buttons, brooches, buckles and necklaces.
Paste: glass made to imitate precious stones.
Pavé setting: the setting of stones side by side with as little metal as possible between the stones.
Pectoral: a plaque worn on the chest. It may be suspended as a pendant or fastened as a brooch.
Pickle: a solution used to clean flux and oxides from metal after heating.
Piercing: cutting with a jeweller's piercing saw.
Pinchbeck: a copper zinc alloy made to imitate gold.
Polyester resin: a synthetic material which can be coloured with transparent or opaque pigments.
Porthos: a coarse abrasive compound sometimes used instead of tripoli.
Refining: the process of extracting the required material from the rough conglomerate.
Repoussé: punching a relief design into metal from the back.
Rolled gold: gold is fused to the surface of a base metal. The two metals are then rolled together into sheets of the required thickness.
Rouge: fine polishing compound used in the final polishing stages.
Shank: that part of a ring which goes around the finger.
Silver: lustrous, white, highly reflective metal. It is both malleable and ductile. Sulphur in the air tarnishes silver, giving it a dark surface discolouration of silver sulphide.
Soldering: hard soldering is the process of joining two pieces of metal with an alloy of the same metal but with a lower melting point. Soft soldering involves the use of a lead-tin solder and is unsuitable for soldering silver and gold.
Solitaire: a ring set with a single stone, usually a diamond.
Specific gravity: the ratio of the weight of a substance to the weight of an equal volume of pure water at standard pressure and a temperature of 4°C.
Stamping: the process of punching out a relief pattern or an outline in metal. The same punch can be used many times, so stamping is suited to the mass production of jewellery.
Steel: iron with added carbon. This enables the metal to be hardened and different quantities of carbon give different qualities of steel. Steel is sometimes made into jewellery, but its most important use is in tools.
Tempering: the process of heating metal to a particular temperature after it has been hardened in order to reduce its brittleness.
Tensile strength: the maximum stress a metal can stand before it breaks.
Texture: an uneven surface.
Triblet: a tapered steel rod used to make rings round.
Tripoli: coarse abrasive used in the first polishing stages.
Troy weight: the system of weight taken from Troyes in France and used to give the weight of precious metal before the introduction of the metric system.
Work hardening: the reduction of the workability of a metal by hammering or bending.

Index

Numbers in italics indicate illustrations.

Credits

Artists
Oxford Illustrators
Ron Hayward Associates
QED

Photographs
Camera Press: 22
Cooper Bridgeman Library: 20
Crown Copyright/Victoria and Albert Museum: 19
Glyn Davies: 26, 29, 33, 38–9, 47, 48, 50, 52, 54, 60, 61, 63, 65, 76–7, 78–9, 80–1
Faillet/Ziolo: 15
Werner Forman: 6
John Freeman/Brian Hunt: 84–5
Michael Holford: contents, 10, 11, 12, 13, 14, 16, 20, 23
Stanley Lechtzin: 72
Mandel/Ziolo: contents
Mansell Collection: 7
The Metropolitan Museum of Art: 15
Museo del Prado: 17 (bottom)
Radio Times Hulton Picture Library: 18, 27
Spectrum Colour Library: 4, 5
Walker Art Gallery: 17 (top)
Wartski: 21
Worshipful Company of Goldsmiths: 18, 21, 23

Cover
Design: Barry Kemp
Photograph: Paul Forrester

Contributing jewellers
All the jewellery appearing in photographs has been lent by students or people who work from small workshops. Any of the pieces could be made at home with the facilities and techniques described in this book.
Gary Cooper: top ring, 33; bottom ring, 54
Stella Doig: enamel tree-brooch, 48
Godfrey Gardiner: pendant, engraved ring, 48; fused rings, 61; on left, 80
Taeko Ishikawa: pearl ring, 48
Bernard Kidd: amethyst ring, 48
John Kitcher: niello brooch, 50
Peter Lamb: rings, 61
Daphne Newble: round enamel pendant, 48
Leonard Pieroni: forged ring, 32; hammered chain, 63; bangle, ebony and ivory pendant, ivory pendant, 65
Jeremy Ross: propeller ring, box ring, mobile bead ring, 60
Suzanne Ross: castings, 76
Teresa Samson: design, painting and pendant, 28-9; leaf necklace, 33
Ester Stevensen: cast ring with diamonds, 77
Sylvia Wicks: design, painting and ring, 28-9; bangle, amethyst brooch, 48; top ring, 54; ring bottom right, 61; chain bottom right, french-knit chain, 63; tortoiseshell brooch, bead pendant, 48; project pieces, 80
Francis Wildt: forged bangle, 33; top pendant, 48; three-gold ring, folded metal ring, 61; two rings cast on right, 77
Brian Wilson: double-link chain top left, 63; African black wood and silver pendant, 65
Sahoko Yoshida: lowest ring, 33